PRAISE FOR CAPS POETRY 2020 AND CAPS SERIES

"In the two decades in which I've been a CAPS fan, I have been wowed time and again by the poets and the poetry of my beloved Hudson Valley. What you hold in your hands is but the tip of a glorious iceberg, but what a refreshing tip it is!"

~ *John Leonard Pielmeier, actor, poet,*
playwright (Agnes of God, The Boys of Winter, Hook's Tale, The Exorcist);
novelist, (Hook's Tale); *screenwriter* (The Pillars of The Earth)

"This anthology captures the vital community of writers living in the Hudson Valley. Calling All Poets over the course of twenty years as evidenced in this volume has nurtured and supported numerous poets, with distinct voices, approaches, styles, and genres. This is a rich and compelling collection of works that speaks deeply to many aspects of the human experience and provides illumination; childhood memories, family relationships, lost love, the search for the meaning in existence, and the witnessing of injustice are all powerfully portrayed. I appreciate the range of form and style from lyric poems to persona and prose poetry, from rich descriptive sensory pieces to philosophical inquiries and surreal and mythic visions. This is a volume that deserves to be read many times, and each time a reader will find new poetic treasures."

Jan Zlotnik Schmidt, SUNY Distinguished Teaching Professor
co-editor of A Slant of Light: Contemporary Women Writers of the Hudson Valley

"Calling All Poets has successfully created a diverse community of poets and writers who support one another. Whenever I'm there, I feel as if I am part of something bigger, a movement in the arts. In addition, they have embraced technology, streaming readers outside the area live and broadcasting the events online. Calling all Poets is the best series in the Hudson Valley!

~ *Rebecca Schumejda, poet*
Cadillac Men, Waiting at the Dead End Diner

"CAPS is about poetry of course. But it's also about community, how it's actually created a community of diverse personalities and backgrounds that come together each month to speak in the one language we all know: The spoken word. Every month there's a mark on the calendar that we all look forward to."

~ *Ken Holland, poet, Pushcart nominee*

"The Hudson Valley boasts a plethora of fascinating poets whose active participation in readings and local events makes them a reliable source of wisdom and inspiration."

~ *Dr. Lucia Cherciu, poet*
Lepădarea de Limbă (The Abandonment of Language)

"The Hudson Valley gives voice to writers and poets who have something of value to say and a comfortable environment for accomplishing this important endeavor. From the caves of Rosendale to the richness of Roost Studios, the Hudson Valley has nurtured me and advanced my career."

~ *Eddie Bell, author, poet*
Capt's Dreaming Chair, Festival of Tears

"The Hudson Valley is one of the most vibrant and exciting poetry regions in the country and Calling All Poets at in Beacon is a centerpiece for the power of words. I feel fortunate to be part of this creative current and to be able to share the art of language with the hundreds of writers I've met and whose works I've been able to read and hear over the years."

~ Laurence Carr, author
Pancake Hollow Primer; *editor:* Reflecting Pool: Poets and the Creative Process and Riverine, *co-editor of* WaterWrites *&* A Slant of Light *(Codhill Press)*

"Thanks to both the many hardworking poetry hosts and the scores of poets who come out to share their work it sometimes seems one could attend a reading every day. And the truly wonderful thing is that the region is home to a number of extremely gifted poets who can leave an audience wishing their reading would never end."

~ Matthew J. Spireng, poet, and three time Pushcart nominee

"I can't imagine living anywhere else in the world. Where else could I find the variety, the devotion, the matter-of-fact respect for poetry not just as an art but a fact of life? From the poetry gangs of Albany to the lost souls of Orange County, I believe the Hudson Valley provides a unique climate for poets of all inclinations to share their work in a supportive environment, a gift not always available to other creators."

~ Cheryl A. Rice, poet
My Minnesota Boyhood, Moses Parts The Tulips

"Generations of painters have drawn inspiration from the age-worn corrugations in Hudson Valley landscapes and the glow of the skies overhead after late-summer thunderstorms give way to dusk. Folk singers impassioned by the rainbow taint of pollutants in the fabled Hudson River gave voice to the modern environmental movement. This latest collection of verse penned by the region's poets—from acidic to comedic to political to pastoral—shows how fertile the ground here is for the written and spoken word, as well. Dive in!"

~ Andy Revkin, longtime environmental journalist, sometime songwriter

"The CAPS Anthology is living proof that poetry, literature and those who continue to create and/or appreciate it are not defined by their location, education, pigmentation or social station. In 2019, The Anthology's home base, the historic Hudson Valley, retains the same magical spirit that inspired 19th Century visual artists to excel and reflect their surroundings. After reading this new collection in the latest CAPS Anthology, we all look forward to MORE!!! Thank you Calling All Poets and all of today's poets for inspiring us and our kids by sharing words and images of lasting value!!"

- David Amram, conductor, composer, and, with Jack Kerouac, the undisputed co-founder of what has become Jazzoetry

"This twentieth anniversary Calling All Poets Anthology consists of some of the best poems by more than forty poets included in the CAPS poetry reading series. The collection is dedicated to Donald Lev (1936-2018) who edited and published Home Planet News, among countless contributions to the literary community. Among the mellifluous vein of talented poets, a sample includes Laurence Carr, Donald Lev, Susan Hoover, Mary Makofske, Roger Aplon, Irene O'Garden, Rebecca Schumejda, Matthew J. Spireng, Lucia Cherciu, Ruth Danon, Bertha Rogers, Jim Eve, Pauline Uchmanowicz, and Mike Jurkovic. This is an anthology that speaks to the current political climate, to nature and climate change, to family dynamics and all phases of human life. Whether shouts or celebrations, prayers or meditations, these poems demonstrate that the Hudson River a shelter for poets and dreamers today just as it once was for Hudson River School painters in the nineteenth century."

~ *Margo Taft Stever, author*
Cracked Piano *(CavanKerry Press, 2019)*

"What if the poets of the Hudson Valley had a party and everybody came? This hospitable and yet lively (read: rockin') anthology catches that spirit. This isn't a Hudson River School of poetry. It's a Hudson Valley lyric line dance. Everyone's invited. Come on down."

~ *TR Hummer, poet*
Eon *(LSU Press, 2018)*, After The Afterlife *(Acre Books, 2018)*,
The Infinity Sessions *(Southern Messenger Poets, 2005)*

"The varied crowd Calling All Poets attracts makes for lively nights. It's rare that we have a dull evening. The fact that the hosts are welcoming and gracious for the presence of a supportive crowd speaks volumes. You don't have nearly the sense of camaraderie anywhere else."

~ *Christopher Wheeling, poet, CAPS photographer*

"I believe that if CAPS continues on the path it is now blazing it will become an important milestone in the growth of American Poetry."

~ *Glenn Werner, poet*
Premeditated Contrition and other poems, *CAPS Tech Czar*

"Poets have grown up at CAPS."

~ *Jim Eve, poet, founder, co-host, Calling All Poets*

CAPS Poetry 2020

20ᵀᴴ ANNIVERSARY

poetry 2020

∽

Edited by
Roger Aplon

Calling All Poets Series
CAPS Poetry 2020 © 2020 by Calling All Poets, Inc., All Rights Reserved

callingallpoets.net

Published by CAPS Press
No part of this book may be reproduced in any form without written permission from the poet. Authors of individual works retain all rights to the poems in this anthology.

Current Venue of Calling All Poets Series (January 2015 to present.)

> The Roost Gallery
> 69 Main Street
> New Paltz, NY 12561

CAPS logo design: Glenn Werner
Photography: Christopher Wheeling
Book design: small packages, inc.

Cover art: Greg Correll

To all the cafés, galleries, cultural centers, libraries, homes, and lounges,
parks—there must be more—oh, yes: bookstores (!) that welcome us,
the poets, and allow us to gather, so that we can meet each other,
try our work, and contribute to the community as only poets can.
And to the hosts and producers of all poetry series
who hold it together even through the
difficulties, trials and tribulations:
this is also dedicated to *you*.

CONTENTS

Prefaces	i	
Introduction	1	Roger Aplon
Dedication	2	
No Exit Ever	3	Donald Lev
Moral Biography	3	Donald Lev
For God's Sake, Look!	4	Donald Lev
Storm	4	Donald Lev
Waiting ...	5	Donald Lev
I See It All Now	5	Donald Lev
In memory of ...	6	
Yankee Swap	7	Pauline Uchmanowicz
Who Knew What When	8	Pauline Uchmanowicz
Bargain Table	9	Pauline Uchmanowicz
Spitting Distance	11	George Wallace
Disturbance of Sleep as a Political Act	12	Walter Worden
Any Death	13	Walter Worden
Refuge In The Storm	14	Davida
Real Lee	16	Penny Wickham Brodie
Walking, Easter	17	Karen Fabiane
Two Lives	18	Richard T. Comerford
her 10th life	20	Laurence Carr
At The Movies	22	Frank Boyer
A Bucket of Bitter Cherries	23	Lucia Cherciu
Alaskan Treasure Chest	24	Judith Saunders
Rural Road, Dusk	26	Matthew J. Spireng
Last Oracle Over The Sea	27	Rayn Roberts
Social Networking	28	Dayl Wise
I Could Tell By The Mustard On My Shirt	29	Dayl Wise

The Museum of Isinglass	30	*Alison Koffler*
Kendra Brings Her Gryphon to School	29	*Alison Koffler*
Turn the Blue Corner	32	*Mike Jurkovic*
Golden Rule	33	*Glenn Werner*
Death By Irony	34	*Steven Hirsch*
Cast-Out ...	36	*Roger Aplon*
Spark	38	*Susan Hoover*
This Poem	39	*Bruce Weber*
Shooting the Dog	40	*Mark Blackford*
Still Looking	42	*Bertha Rogers*
Blocked	43	*Jim Eve*
I Think You Were In My Dream	44	*Peter Ullian*
Taking Out a Comma	46	*Leslie Gerber*
She Says	48	*Catherine Arra*
Reincarnation by Street Light	50	*Christopher Wheeling*
Against Dawn	51	*Joann Deiudicibus*
Eleven and a Half Years	52	*Marianna Boncek*
Taking Flight	54	*Guy Reed*
Riverfront Green Park, Peekskill	55	*T. G. Vanini*
Blue Balloon	56	*Louisa Finn*
blot or the one percent	57	*Marina Mati*
The House	58	*Susan Konz*
Sergeant Eleanor Is Laid To Rest	60	*Irene O'Garden*
Coffee Break	62	*Michael Sean Collins*
Vicious Ending	64	*Gregory Wilder*
First Day of Autumn	65	*John Martucci*
Corrected Versions	66	*Greg Correll*
Cabbage	68	*William Seaton*
The April Showers Gate	69	*Sharon Ferrante*
Henri Rousseau Answers Questions	70	*Raphael Kosek*
The Sunflower	71	*Linda Lerner*
Solitaire	72	*Lewis Gardner*

Evasion	73	*Ruth Danon*
Spellbound	74	*Janet Hamill*
At Any Given…	75	*Janet Hamill*
Catskill Thunder	76	*Teresa Costa*
Trevor and the Pterodactyl	77	*Donna Reis*
This Country Could Break My Heart	78	*Mary Makofske*
Variations on a Line from The New York Times	79	*Mary Makofske*
Between Daylight And The Deep	80	*Mary Newell*
The Rub	81	*Susan Chute*
Sepia Life	82	*Ken Holland*
Home	84	*Ken Holland*
Catalogue	85	*Timothy Brennan*
Father	86	*Yuyutsu Sharma*
November, so we leave nothing but the bones	88	*Scott Bankert*
Hirundo Rustica	89	*Scott Bankert*
Half Assed Pegasus	90	*Gary Siegel*
Walking My Dog During a Florida Thunderstorm	92	*Dennis Wayne Bressack*
My Friend Che	93	*R. Dionysius Whiteurs*
Got Caught Up In Out	94	*Edwin Torres*
Love Jones	95	*Eddie Bell*
Dream The Night John Lennon Was Shot	96	*Tim Tomlinson*
A Poem About Our Fuck Last Wednesday	98	*Tim Tomlinson*
Death Is A White Catfish	99	*Shotsie Gorman*
The Whole Crowd	100	*Fred Poole*
Happy As A Lark?	101	*Fred Poole*
A Catholic Girlhood in Queens	102	*Ron Kolm*
Breasts	103	*Cheryl A. Rice*
The Visit	104	*Marta Szabo*
The Nieves Flores Library, Guam	106	*Fr. Bob Phelps*
Rue	107	*Pamela Twining*

The Circus	108	*Tara Yetter*
Then He Begged Me to Go Back with Him and Rescue the Others	110	*Rebecca Schumejda*
When Wind is not Enough	111	*Rebecca Schumejda*
Striding	112	*Addison Goodson*
PoetryPrompt.com	113	*Matthew Hupert*
Advice to a Young Poet from Your Uncle in Canarsie	114	*Will Nixon with Mike Jurkovic*
Career Advice from Your Uncle in Canarsie	115	*Will Nixon with Mike Jurkovic*
Family Tree	116	*Thom Francis*
Listerine	117	*Thom Francis*
Her Lot	118	*Kate Hymes*
The Poets	*121*	

"Poetry is not only a dream and vision;
it is the skeleton architecture of our lives.
It lays the foundations for a future of change,
a bridge across our fears of what has never been before."

Audre Lorde

"A poet's work is to name the unnamable, to point at frauds,
to take sides, start arguments, shape the world,
and stop it going to sleep."

Salman Rushdie

"Poetry lifts the veil from
the hidden beauty of the world, and
makes familiar objects be as if they were not familiar."

Percy Bysshe Shelley

PREFACES

Did anyone attending that first open mic in March '99 think it would result in this celebratory anthology and a community of world class poets? I for one wasn't there, but Original Pessimist that I am, I'd say more than likely not. But alas, here we are, thanks to the many voices and visions presented in this volume and the many more who have made the mic their own over the last two decades.

But other wonderfulness happened in those 7300 days fulfilling CAPS larger or, some might say, delusional vision. Perseverance, determination and our deep cell, human need for connection have made it the longest running, most diverse and dynamic poetry series in the Mid-Hudson Valley. CAPS has become a poetry hub, an expansive network connecting poets from New York, Long Island, Woodstock, Albany, New Jersey, Pennsylvania, Nepal, California, and Connecticut. And with todays's technology, CAPS reaches further into the global community, streaming our events live and sometimes streaming poets in for readings from around the world.

How frikkin' cool is that?! Who thought that twenty years ago?

As Jim is fond of saying, "Poets grow up at CAPS." And now we can taste the fine cabernet whose varietals include acclaimed playwright/poet/memoirist Pushcart Award winner Irene O'Garden and world renowned tattoo artist/poet Shotsie Gorman. Author/poet/photographer Eddie Bell, poet/translator William Seaton, and performance poet Janet Hamill. Regional Poet Laureates, Poet Gold, Peter Ullian, Raphael Kosek and Suffolk County's first poet laureate and internationally recognized poet, George Wallace mic drop frequently. Albany Poets President Thom Francis can be heard. National Slam winner Elizabeth K. Gordon visits regularly. Yuyutsu Sharma, the world traveling poetry ambassador from Nepal, stops by First Friday at the Roost whenever he's in the metro area.

CAPS includes award winning poets: Rebecca Schumejda, Mary Makofske, Ken Holland, Andy Clausen, and Matthew J. Spireng. Pushcart Nominees include Glenn Werner and yours truly. Regional publishers include Dayl Wise and Alison Kofler (Post Traumatic Press) and Jane Ormerod (great weather for media) are regulars. From the English and Writing Departments of SUNY and Marist we have Dr. Lucia Cherciu, Larry Carr, Jan Schmidt, Joann K. Deiudicibus, and recent NYU retiree Ruth Danon.

And sadly, we must acknowledge the passing of our good friends Don Lev and Pauline Uchmanowicz.

Besides numerous books bearing their names, CAPS supporters Fred Poole, Will Nixon, Kate Hymes, Dan Wilcox, Roberta Gould, Cheryl Anne Rice, Ron Kolm, Linda Lerner and a host of others publish regularly on the national level. 2017 CUNY Fellow and CLIO award winner Greg Correll calls CAPS home and makes sure www.callingallpoets.net stays current. Poet and official photographer/archivist Christopher Wheeling has an uncanny way of making us all look good. And, as we prepare this anniversary anthology, Beacon poet, publisher, and guest editor Roger Aplon features CAPS poets in his nationally distributed magazine, the bi-annual Waymark—Voices of the Valley.

Our active website www.callingallpoets.net, Facebook page (*facebook.com/callingallpoetsseries*), YouTube (*youtube.com/channel/UCbTkXI6QILPcHY8PDuhCoxg*), SoundCloud (*soundcloud.com/calling-all-poets*) serve to further showcase the artistic integrity that sustains Calling All Poets. CAPS Press—you are reading our third publication—expands our reach further still. Word of mouth from poets and patrons continues to bring people to our First Friday readings at Roost Studios in New Paltz, our monthly open mic at the Towne Crier Cafe in Beacon, our JazzOetry events at Quinn's in Beacon, and special events at the Denizen Theater in New Paltz. And let's not forget our Ekphrasis Project, the continuing collaboration with Roost Studios (*roostcoop.org*) scheduled to exhibit February - March 2020.

This is who we are and who we'll continue to be: an open forum for novice and veteran voices alike, guaranteeing the democratization of free speech. A special place where words and language bear meaning, not noise and division. Twenty years of community. CAPS@20.

Give yourselves a hand.

~ Mike Jurkovic
Producer and Host, CAPS Jazzoetry at Quinn's and PPD
Producer and Co-Host, the Calling All Poets Series

March 1, 2019 marked the 20th anniversary of the Calling All Poets Series. What started out as a simple desire to host a poetry reading twenty years ago turned into so much more. CAPS back then and even today has been about the poets who through the spoken word create and share their art with others.

Their participation in CAPS as a reader, be it a feature or open mic'er, contributor, member, or volunteer or donor, has carried CAPS and sustained CAPS over the years. Mike Jurkovic, a dear friend and partner and myself could not have managed the program over the years without the contribution of the many.

I want to thank all that have contributed, supported and participated in CAPS those 20 years. There are many. The list is long. But without you there would be no CAPS. This 20th Anniversary CAPS Anthology is for all that have been a part of CAPS through those years. My personal thanks to Mike Jurkovic, Greg Correll, Christopher Wheeling, Glenn Werner, Marina Mati, Marcy Bernstein and the Roost Studios and Art Gallery.

To every poet that has come through the doors of CAPS wherever we resided, "Thank You."

~ Jim Eve
Founder and Co-Host, the Calling All Poets Series

Though I wasn't at the very first CAPS reading, I must have started going sometime during its first year. I've always felt a strong loyalty for CAPS and consider my relationship with it to be a major highlight of my life. Early on I began designing Fliers for CAPS events and soon had the honor of designing the CAPS logo. During that time I think I grew as a poet, using the opportunity CAPS gave for me to try out new work and see what worked and what didn't.

I am most proud of my time as The CAPS organization's Vice President and being part the planning and execution of its new and innovative events and programs like the Ekphrasis Project, Jazzquerade and Jazzoetry events that have expanded CAPS' involvement in the Hudson Valley literary scene. These accomplishments are dear to me beyond words. I trust CAPS will go on for many more twenty year milestones.

~ Glenn Werner

I made all the usual mistakes when I first started to read my work. Not looking at the audience, mumbling in a monotone, afraid to emote. I got impatient, waiting to read, and was anxious to leave when I was done.

Great writing penetrated, though. Took me out of myself, inspired me, set a bar for my own poetry. Over the years, listening at CAPS, all writing began to matter, because I learned to listen on more than one level. To hear what was intended, not just the attempt.

I was too critical, and worked on my half-assed Buddhism.

In Ben Lerner's *The Hatred of Poetry*, he explains the inevitable failure of all poets, all poetry, to meet expectations. And how to change expectations, go deeper.

I learned to respect, to *love*, anyone brave enough to scribble lines, much less stand and read—and I learned this at CAPS. To love the effort and feeling, whether the craft was there or not. To admire the craft, when the heart of a poem was obscured. To feel ecstatic when a poet's work contained everything: polish and ability, original choices, ineffable soul.

And to expect it, from CAPS poets.

~ Greg Correll

INTRODUCTION

It's been an honor & a privilege to edit the 20th anniversary anthology for CAPS. Jim, Mike, Glenn, & Greg have built one of the most prestigious poetry series in New York State, equal to & even surpassing those I've witnessed across the country. The poems I've had the pleasure to read for this anthology were in some cases risky, but always inventive, thoughtful & emotionally enriching. I'm certain, after you've had time to engage the entire collection, you too will be as appreciative as am I, of the eclectic range of styles, voices & focus.

Over the past sixty-plus years American Poetry has dramatically transitioned from the academy to the street. That transition has been accompanied by explorations in form, language & content previously frowned upon. With that transition came a titillating array of fresh sounds & radiant colors never before considered by more traditional interpreters of our homegrown 'verse.'

Between these covers you'll find many examples of risk-taking that's comfortably at home with more or less anticipated forms. Over all, I find the quality extraordinary. That said, it is my pleasure to have been able to collect & present the best of CAPS. To all who submitted for this anniversary collection, I say, Thank You. There's great stuff here – Please engage & enjoy it.

~ *Roger Aplon, Editor*
June 2020

DEDICATION: DONALD LEV

It was about ten days before he passed on September 30, 2018 when I last spoke with Donald.

He was, gratefully, having a good day. The prior few months had been hard. Hospital, rehab, hospital, nursing home, hospital . . . He was in good spirits. We laughed. He told me he sorely missed coming to CAPS but that he just couldn't climb the stairs anymore.

And that's when it hit me that persistence was Donald Lev's great truth and his lasting gift to us all. Persistence to create, to laugh, to love, to write. To live! Born in New York in 1936, he drove cabs, went to Hunter, worked wire rooms for the Daily News and New York Times. He ran messages through the Lower East Side's tangled streets. He ran the Home Planet Bookstore. He was the cabbie/poet in Putney Swope. He persisted through the great love affair with Enid Dame (1943-2003) and her illness. Together they ran Home Planet News.

His first published poems were in 1958. His last just a few months before his passing. "Persistence," the Apostle John writes in Romans, "gives character." And Donald most certainly was.

No Exit Ever
  for Phil Levine

Hell isn't only other people, it is also no other people.
Jean Paul Sartre and his cool ilk
fabricated an existential hero alone
in glacial subterranea
making cool decisions because
he had no choice but choice.
I am enjoying such freedom, nowadays.
I wished myself a happy (don't laugh)
69th birthday at a bar with gibsons and
steak sandwich. Only my second in the last
27 I was not across a table from the one
other person that had been my heaven.
Cool existentialist poet that I was I
guess I gave little inkling on paper all those years
on how it really was.

5/15/05

              from *Grief* (Bardpress/Ten Penny Players, 2006)

Moral Biography

He was a bad man,
Stalin,
Though he loved to sing.

1/12/18

Donald Lev

For God's Sake, Look!

i put my
coat
over my head, my
hat floated
a few inches above that, so
it appeared to
the casual observer that
i was without a head,
which is ridiculous.
my head being where
my heart beat,
under my coat.

from *There Is Still Time* (The Poet's Press, 1986)

Storm

Help! The sky is filled with falling books!
The sun is hidden by them.
They are crashing wildly all over the prairie destroying
   farmhouses,
Barns, stables and radio stations.
They are flattening new crops, destroying whole
   agra businesses.
Chickencoops are crushed. Feathers fly among the pages.
When and where will it end? What will it mean
When all the land lies quiet under blankets of
   unread books?

from *Yesterday's News* (CRS Outloudbooks, 2002)

Waiting …

for what?
for the other shoe to drop?
for the tide to rise and fall?
for the image of the Void
to reproduce itself beneath my breast bone?

i have waited for happiness,
for surfeit of pleasure,
for surcease of sorrow.

i have waited for robins. i have waited for snow.

i wait for you now
so I won't have to wait alone.

from *Enemies of Time* (Warthog Press, 2000)

I See It All Now

I see it all now.
I don't know where I've been
That I've been deluded so long.

Now it's clear.
You readers and hearers,
You've always known.

1/7/18

IN MEMORY OF
PAULINE UCHMANOWICZ

Pauline Uchmanowicz was my mentor, colleague, and friend. My favorite mornings began when she'd come by my desk and say, "Hey, pal! Do you want to read some poems?" Then, we'd abandon our work to share recent drafts. She gave everything, especially to writing, meticulously carving her poems to a core image—precise moments artfully rendered in the microcosm of an almost-first kiss or the macrocosm of sky/seascapes. Pauline's unfaltering love to create poetry taught me what is possible, both in language and in life. May her words move us.

~ Joann K. Deiudicibus

Pauline Uchmanowicz, author of poetry collection Starfish (2016), directed the Creative Writing Program at SUNY New Paltz. Her work has appeared in Commonweal, Crazyhorse, Indiana Review, Ploughshares, and elsewhere. She always appreciated the generosity of spirit encountered at Calling All Poets events, which feature big-hearted audiences alongside writers whose words sear then linger in the imagination.

Yankee Swap

Will trade your one hundred and ten
Fahrenheit in the shade, air conditioning

out of order brownout, for my ice storm
skating rink driveway, my cardinal

beating against windows like an aggrieved
heart, for your steeple soundless as snow.

As for creed and color, let's not unburden
one another. We've gotten what we've gotten.

Hole-punched or sucker punched. Swaddled
in prayer flags or the red-white-and-blue.

Pauline Uchmanowicz

Who Knew What When

Buzzards Bay had a temperature.
Highest in twenty years.

Alligators in Florida parking lots
Terrorized locked cars. Touring

Hurricanes blew shingles off
Too-late-to-divest rooftops.

Mortgages went bust. Foreclosure
Vultures circled. Jobs were lost.

Handguns purchased. End-times
Prophesized. Climate change foretold.

How to skin and dress an animal
Relearned. How to tie a fishhook.

Bargain Table

Dusk at a rummage sale,
the final browser, lifting up
a star-spangled colander,
uncovers an ounce of mercy
in nearly perfect condition,
previous owners having stored it
for special occasions only,
deep within darkened closets
next to piled suitcases
intended for quick escapes
that never materialized.

Roused to fuller attention,
the vendor quotes his
discounted price, then,
sensing buyer's hesitation,
inquires whether the customer
might like to acquire
a slightly soiled but
seldom paged-through
complete set of cardinal virtues.

Pauline Uchmanowicz

Spitting Distance

here is a man within spitting distance of glory or death
- ready to leap blind as a butterfly into the sun - a man
at the precipice, a man in the heart of the kaleidoscope,
a question mark, an affirmation, a quick calculation, a man
not knowing, what do we know of spring or love or trans-
formation, a blind resume of a man, a man who fights too
little or too much, with society with honor with god, with
oblivion and with himself, always with himself, a man at
the center and at the edge, the earth moves under his feet
like water, it moves for all men, he is no more no less than
a man who wakes to a dream of being awake - endless
work to go sleepwalking along the palisades, to consider
the consequences, take in the extremes - here is a man
cashing in his chips, casting his bones before his body,
here are the risks, his trusty brain goes tick-tock, distance,
impact, trajectory, flow, yes here is a man embracing the
densities, he is ready for metamorphosis, he's putting
hesitation aside, stripping off, here's the shape of a shape-
shifting man—i am dazzling sunlight, i am life pulse
in shadow, i am river racing beneath my own two feet—
here is the art of a man, a man translating doubt, so
much love, so much love, upriver snow is falling, down-
river the deluge - here he is huddled in his over-
clothes, here is the plunge, the river! now he is at the
center of the thing, this is the vortex, no not in a hurry,
river take your time, a man takes his time, all the ice and
urgency, nothing! it's all about the magnetics, there's your
currency, his father told him, when the old man was alive &
among us, with snow on his shoulders and fire in his eyes

George Wallace

Disturbance of Sleep as a Political Act

Forgive the force
of my shaking
your arm,
or the brusque
and brutish manner
of my shouting up the stairs,
or the blinding
brightness of the light
in your eyes that cuts
through the consoling dark.
Forgive me
if I have gone too far
by not bringing you
a continental breakfast.
Forgive me for the banging drum.
I only wanted to wake you.

Any Death

for Donald Lev

A death—any death—
is also each of ours,
a little of ourselves going
along until what is finally left,
what hangs on to the last breath,
is the center of what we are,
what keeps us whole in the interim
between one death and another.

Sometimes a quiet man of words
must out of anguish and want of rescue,
wrap his relentless grief in leaves of verse,
better to haul the disconsolate load
through the long length of years,
comfort achieved by the miracle of craft.

Such an isolate wayfarer, though meeting
many of his kind enroute, must
of necessity, travel the cold, stygian winter
by his own lamp, the light of which reaches
no clear path, yet shows the way to warmth
mile by mile, step by step, poem by little poem,
until with grace the words give out, and he arrives.

Walter Worden

Davida

Refuge In The Storm

Before we expected the hurricane (Floyd in the late 90's), which spun off random tiny tornadoes whizzing through Woodstock homes and forests at hummingbird speeds, my best friend and fellow psychic Chris Pearce called from Minneapolis and said to me "I smell pine all around you..".

We weren't clear on what that meant, or when, but I had the impression of a near or beyond death experience..

A few days later, hurricane warnings flew by and when it was beginning, I thought I'd like to get away from the water, out from under the trees.. and not be alone, but with friends while weathering the storm. Although there were many friends, even within walking distance, I could not think of anyone to call.. and then the storm came in full swing.. water rising, trees bending.. objects flying in dark torrential winds..

Eventually, seeping into my downstairs quarters, the stream water was swelling into the yard, up toward my living room. I unplugged things and went upstairs to hunker in my loft space with my feline companion; another best friend... my closest best friend, Sheema. Although we knew this was a dangerous situation, I felt a deep sense of safety. Cozied in, even as Sheema purred, a falling tree hit the roof of the low ceiling just above our heads. The entire house shook, but the roof did not break.

Immediately the phone rang. We hadn't spoken in over a week, but Chris was totally tuned in and started telling me jokes, keeping me laughing, even to tears throughout most of the event, which lasted for hours. deep Into the howling night of the trees cracking. We would take a break and he'd call back to continue.. I had brought some food upstairs, Sheema and I had an extra bathroom there; all our amenities and needs met.. even after the electric and phone went out as the hurricane stormed screeched, hollered and whistled with many voices through the hamlet of Woodstock..

I thought of the monks up on top of the mountain at the Tibetan Monastery.. knew they were ok; sent them a blessing prayer. I still don't know why I didn't think to go up there with Sheema.. I know Khenpo Karthar Rinpoche would have been happy to see us and was sending blessings.

The next day in the beaming sunlight, I went out to see the wreckage. My townhouse uninjured, the home next door had it's roof destroyed under the broken tree that was leaning on my roof. Across the street two houses up the way, bed, artwork, furniture, wide open to public view; a house split cleanly by a tall old pine which had fallen across the road, taking the lines down with it. The couple had been out of town. Peering through some parts of the woods, there were newly clear-cut whirly-trails of fallen trees where some of the tornados had broken out and traversed.

Standing in my yard by the stream who was rushing over the rocks laughing and sparkling, breathing in the crystalline air I realized.. I was surrounded by the scent of pine..

Penny Wickham Brodie

Real Lee

"Good and Plenty."
"Hot Stuff."
Titles of cookbooks stacked on the bench
So the pianist can sit and play.

And she is hot stuff
And plays good jazz
And plenty of it
At 88 years old.

Bassist over her left shoulder
Smooth and sincere on a deconstructed instrument
Just right for a small jazz corner
So fans can draw near.

He aware of her every nuance, cue.
A lift of the shoulder, a turn of her head, a cast of the eyes
Signaled many musical maneuvers:
Stroll, lay out, trade, solo, chase me, take it home baby.

No need for scores.
A call and a nod is 'nuff said due to
Years of jamming in all kinds of sets
With almost anybody, on almost any tune.

 Lee Shaw is her name
That's right. Lee Shaw is her name.
And I've heard of her many times over the years.
I wish I dug her sooner.

There she is. Still creating.
Fingers bouncing on keys releasing
Notes so crisp and riffs so flawless.
Sittin' on cookbooks to command the scene!

You'd better listen up. Keep up.
The teacher's talkin'.

Walking, Easter

The streets seem the same.
Unblemished
by the patina of saintliness,
but the fishers are out, @ the canal just footsteps
from my door, casting/using nets
for trout, as they do this time every year. But not too many
today. Church bells

@ 9 AM only. Not so long ago, calls to Easter Mass rang out earlier
& later, @ least three times by noon,
+ a late ceremony around 4 PM. Yet the bells
sounding thru my windows further pacified the morning, slow
& bright & easy, no miracle
but resembling peace, a gentle going back
to conventions I (Presbyterian heathen transformed to lapsed Pagan)

never shared. The bell's ringing assumes no holy
overlay, only resonates
to a past made more gentle by memory,
of a time made from different customs, now seemingly gone
forever, & never really as good
as one recalls.

The streets seem
the same; no more church bells but vegetation appearing
where last week there was none ~~ backyards (I
walk the alleys), trees becoming
green with new life. Along the whole path
only one met, a woman (about my age) pruning
a growth of brambles
@ her property's outer edge; she say "hi."

No fat angels nor skinny saints; neither also
holy guy waking
from the dead; just the miracle of being here
a little longer.

Karen Fabiane

Richard T. Comerford

Two Lives

We are creatures of summer,
Living and growing for such a short time.
But we make the most of it,
Because we know winter will come again
—what a bummer.
We shed the heavy clothes,
Exchange them for cut-offs and jeans.
The bike is uncovered,
And we're ready to ride again.
The ol' lady also transforms.
From a shapeless mass of clothes
To that darling that lies beneath.
In all her glory, down to her toes.
Running wild and free,
How can we live such a life many people think?
No home for days
Living on the brink.
Home is a garage filled with tools.
A refrigerator in the corner,
Stocked with plenty of beer.
We're often called a pair of fools.
The bike is torn down,
Money is tight.
New tires and plugs, maybe some new paint.
Working to get it just right.
We live on our unemployment,
While building the bike.
We eat beans and bacon,
Going to town for parts, even if I have to hike.
But another life awaits us,
Come spring we'll shed our cocoons.
We'll blossom into another self,
It just can't happen too soon.

When you live for the desire,
To hear the bikes thunder in your ears
The wind is a caress,
Dearer than any lover can inspire.
Chilled and wet through,
Sun burnt and wind swept,
Tired and hungry
We're in nobody's debt.
Don't look back,
Ride hard, die fast.
And don't compromise,
It's our life to the last.
We shovel snow and stoke the stove,
Or sit and listen to the rain.
But we're happy together
And endure the pain.

Richard T. Comerford

Laurence Carr

her 10th life

her shadow floats
across the rug diffused
through west bay sunsets

and for a moment
she's a presence until
the moment when she isn't

I see her—but it's only
a pile of sock strewn
laundry on the closet floor

I hear her in the midnight
creak of floorboards that
catch her tone and timbre

phantoms live among us
more comfortable with you
than you with them

she has no thought of leaving
no reason really
and little inclination

this house has always been
more hers than mine
she owns the deed

and time which
ticks me off is no longer
part of her routine

she has ceased to be an
earthbound wanderer
content in her nonworld

Laurence Carr

she no longer lifts soft paws
but glides from room to room
her footsteps even lighter now

a shade of former self
an imprint a remembrance
of all she ever was and all
she is and all she leaves behind

At The Movies

All along Nightmare Alley *Hurry! Hurry!* Step this way! troopers are reeling in the rubes. Right in front, all T & T, Miss Zena tippy-toes the wire. *Watch out! Watch out! Over there!* Crimson feathers fly! "Omygod! He's ripping a chicken apart alive!" *Ladies and Gentlemen! Man or beast!?* Hell, it's only the Geek. *This way! This way! Over here! Through the curtain. You? Afraid? Hurry! Hurry! Right this way...*

Between Miss Zena's hands the tarot cards parade. Faith strikes in the highest places. Addicted to miracles, the Doctor pulls a gun. The Geek walks by, singing like a ricochet. Again the tarot cards flash and fall and rearrange. Faith on strike! Words spill out of books, swarm like army ants, devour Love's body and carry it away.

From the Magician's dead soul, another Geek is born. "I'll do anything," he says. He knows the part. Drunk with the bums, he rolls his sleepless face in midnight muck. Hollow Geek screams scald his throat.

A black man wrestles her gun from Zena's hand. The Geek runs through the carnival night, shrieks with the train that means the end, as through the Blue Angel's dressing room, the Professor wanders. The Space Clown passes, humming Wagner. Lola languidly doffs her costume, redolant with mastery. Figures on the coo coo clock dance in and out of doors. "Catch us if you can!" they sing. The Professor cleans his glasses with Lola's underwear. Oh, oh, oh! Bring in the polka dots and ruff! He's ready to play Clown! He'll lay an egg and flap and crow, 'cause after all, Faith strikes in the highest places...

Even here, last balcony row, I share a kiss and I'm ready to risk my dreams. *Come on! Let's go! Into the sunset with Charlot!*

Long shot, jump cut—we're out the door, running through night streets carnivals coo coo clocks shooting miracles shooting stars shouting *"Hart Crane for President! Charlie Chaplin is King!"*

Frank Boyer

A Bucket of Bitter Cherries

The old man went to pick black cherries, managed to fill
two buckets, but then had a hard time carrying them

back home, more than twenty-five pounds each.
He managed for a while, but when he got to the creek

he left one of them on the side of the road, in a prominent
place, for someone to find it, because there was no way

he could have climbed the steep path up on the hill
with all the cherries weighting him down. At eighty-seven

he was lucky enough to walk, he laughed to himself,
but kept turning to see the lone bucket left behind,

all the pies, the plum brandy he could add them to
for taste and color, or make wine with them, spend the day

canning preserves, as if his summer too was in that valley,
sitting on the bank of that creek.

Lucia Cherciu

Alaskan Treasure Chest
[mixed media]

Filled with tourist treasure, jumbled
park brochures and maps, wildlife
guidebooks, photographs and postcards,
ticket stubs from ferries, trains, museums,
this miniature wooden pirate's chest
cannot contain Alaska—big
boisterous 49th state.

Denali has poked its icy peak
through the lid, straining skyward
in full color. Fantastical salmon,
Juno's answer to Chicago's Cow Parade,
have swum through cracks in the sides,
somersaulting nonchalantly
across one blue-stained panel.

Native carvings and figurines—
Yupnik, Inupiac, Haida—
have staked their claim front and back.
A feather-trimmed, ancient face of horn
shapes its mouth in astonishment.
A mermaid of the North—half-woman,
half seal—drifts by on walrus bone.

A staring, soapstone crone displays
her ever fertile, bright-green bosom.
On a slab of darkened antler
patiently etched, a massive bear
observes two spouting whales
while line-on-line-on-line conjures
silence: ocean, cloud, black sun.

Through the one remaining panel
of the still unopened chest, a stream
has forced its way; someone is panning
there for gold. Sled dogs, too,
have escaped from the interior,
a circle of friendly muzzles and fur
with you at its smiling center.

first published in Lost Partners *(FutureCycle Press, 2015)*

Matthew J. Spireng

Rural Road, Dusk

The sun is setting
and though it is late May
it feels autumnal—cumulus clouds
threatening rain, light gusts of wind

and last night in the thirties—
and a farmer is still out
plowing a field, seven
or eight more passes

before he is done and can
climb down out of the seat
and go in where dinner waits
to be warmed over.

Now, though, he is intent
on finishing, turning the whole field
of stubble corn to dark
moist earth ready for planting.

Last Oracle Over The Sea

You ask a moment from a singing spirit of reasoning light
in the prison and heaving heaven of the heart I give

an enigma darkened by wheel rut days, renegade nights
a body pulsing in shadowy houses collapsing, ruined.

From a life in the space stars make while burning I give
a plea for a crossing of bright water, a linked sea to sail

silver-grey waves, an hour without the trap of tomorrow
closing down on all unknowing new, old migrating souls

innocent, yet sentenced to be, taken by fatal, sad surprise
like prey in the black eye of a great white, you ask an oracle

I say in reply, name from what void rising in blood we come
to what destination pushing away bones do we return and

what are we here, consumed in heat of seasons, tangled
in a net of hours, touching a river as boats sway setting out

I give you the universe for nothing, nothing for all you own
darkness riddled with moth holes, fire rising from the sea

Rayn Roberts

Social Networking

Ho Chi Minh requested my friendship on Facebook today.
In an instant message he thanked me for my friendship
said he liked my poetry, but I think he was just being nice, most
Vietnamese are. He has twelve friends, most of them dead.

Ho reconnected with his first wife, Zeng, a Chinese woman,
through Facebook who just retired after a long career as a midwife.
Said he still loved her, was sorry he left her, but she is happily married.
She unfriended him. Uncle Ho is very depressed, his heart broken.

Ho now lives in Brooklyn, travels by bike to Battery Park to sell
red tee shirts with his likeness in a yellow star made in Viet Nam.
Other novelty items include Richard Nixon and Bob Hope
bobblehead dolls. No one recognizes Ho as he sits there smiling

drinking sticky rice wine.

I Could Tell By The Mustard On My Shirt

that we were at Playland. In this dream
on the boardwalk, my mom, long dead,
holds my hand, smokes a cigarette with the other.

Another night, perhaps late summer, we're at
Rye Beach, building sand castles, holding off jellyfish,
horseshoe crabs and other sea-monsters.

I'm tethered to a cloud to limit my range of movement, but still
able to man the castle walls with my Betty Boop sand bucket
and red plastic shovel to turn back evil in the incoming tide.

Mom under her umbrella looks up over her magazine,
good boy and puffs her Virginia Slim. And me,
still on the wall, scanning the beach for trouble.

Dayl Wise

Alison Koffler

The Museum of Isinglass

It's time to enter.
Bring pennies from
the eyelids of the dead.
Bring the stubs of your candles.

The museum has many doors.
Avoid the Hall of Thorns and
the Room of the Cyclops Lamb.
Run swiftly through
the Corridor of Wolves.

Beneath a trap door
in the museum's basement
lies the earth's navel.
You may not be ready.
Wait at the bronze cash register.
Pick up the bone flute.
Play it or remain silent.

You can pick up the boxes
of buttons and brass keys,
porcupine quills wrapped in silk,
the zebra beetle cupped in a bell jar,
a jasper hand axe fitted to your palm.

Take off your clothes and notice
how naked you are. Place the crown
of antlers on your head. Wrap yourself
in a cloak of mica, feathers and fish skin,
stripe your forehead with red ochre,
tie bells to your wrists to welcome
the wilderness in.

Kendra Brings Her Gryphon to School

No one else is able to see him, not even
the cops by the metal detectors, or the
scary big boys. Kendra rests her hand

on the gryphon's steel-feathered shoulder
as they head for the stairs. The hall is a riot
of voices, kids running, teachers yelling.

The gryphon twists his head to look
at her with fierce bird eyes. In math,
he sprawls alertly under her desk.

Struggling vainly with long division,
she rests one sneaker on his haunch.
The teacher drones. Her gryphon quietly

flicks his foliate tail. In the corner,
three girls she doesn't know toss papers
out the window. Maria and Tromaine

are busy texting. Tenzin gnaws his pencil.
Clumps of toilet tissue cling to the ceiling.
Her gryphon yawns.

Kendra admires his curled black tongue
and lion paws, the metallic glint of his primaries
as he stretches his wings, huge among the chairs.

The boys in the back wouldn't talk so bad
if they could see him watching them
with gilded, predatory eyes.

Alison Koffler

Mike Jurkovic

Turn the Blue Corner

Caught in the rhythm
of the Great American Thimblerig
I find myself shuffling shells
for the tourists from Wisconsin
Who missed their bus
and now they're here. On Avenue C,
Where all the psychosis
slides east on Thursdays
Asking themselves
or someone else
or someone
just as fucked
If the two drink minimum
applies to them.

Everything pertains in New York
I say. So throw some hot sauce
on that plain cheese pizza
and watch carefully.
The night remains sleepless
and it makes no difference
What language the ole lady yells
when she wanted
Ranch, you asshole! Not hot sauce!

Golden Rule

We have all negotiated
A painful road to its end,

And though we handled it,
We handled it poorly.

We cannot be up to every test
Nor wave our banner in any gale.

If the world looked in on us then
Would they not scoff and blame?

If we are to expect
our trespasses to be forgiven,

We then are bonded to
Forgive those who trespass.

We all shelter some secret failure,
Seek absolution without inquisition.

Only we alone were there
To know the virtues of our weakness.

Our deepest truth? Our frailty.
And sin, our first honest act.

Glenn Werner

Death By Irony

When up against the wall
if you look very closely at it cross-eyed
you may see its future absence taking shape
when all obstacles are cleared
and your horse is lead into the sun by reins of gilt iron and Elk hide.
And, then again, you may see a dead horse up against the wall,
its grey teeth shine in the white sun.
As you ride into town everyone cries "Fuck you and the dead horse
      you rode in on!"

Work/life balance is a plane in a nosedive spin toward inevitability.

The weight of your own thoughts crushes you. Spontaneity is lost. You desperately try to hang on to your sanity and composure but the situation just keeps getting more desperate; you knew it was coming, you knew, you could have predicted it. You got what you expected. A fist. Carpet pulled from under Atlas.

Twist of the wrist down 208 past the prison with everyone and their cousin's slo-go motorhome making for one sad motor like a 300-baud modem, slow and hot boredom watching lights. I sliced the 10-ball into the corner pocket and decided not to ride to Kingston for bad burgers & smell of Gorilla Snot and a ride home down the Thruway with the Sunday race home from the country crowd. Anger, Rage and Sadness on vacation, returning home to prison and Parker rolls.

Patience, patience, child, first learn to flush the toilet, then we'll talk about world domination. After all it's got to be a stepwise journey, a juggling act that that you must prove you can handle. That's right just pull the handle, there you go. Now jump up on that unicycle and I'll pass you my mismatched batons. The luminance of a radiant mind runs wild down unintended paths from time to time when time is not what we think but what we are as we decide.

Always at a crossroads or a threshold
the reason or benefit escapes me
the minor and the major agree
there is no harmony without transition
and nothing can relate to its opposite
without suspense and tension.

Salary rises with stress and
there's no separate devil from the Samboghakaya illusion-body details
Endless images that form in the darkness before dawn keep the
unformed potential in play, imagination fasts to purge comfort and ennui,
image gets thin and brighter as you waste away into suchness.

You become the Enterprise Architect at the midwestern bar
building a tower of empty cans and powerpoint slides.
A spark of unborn insight sweeps in from the right.
You slide off the barstool—cold hand grips celphone
knuckles ashen white.

Steven Hirsch

Cast-Out...

Cast-out. Castaway. Casual. Cunning. Cruel. Corrupt. Candid. Condensed. Condescend. Cornered. Covered. Corny. Clever.

On the other hand. From her backhand you'd think . . . Stranded. Startled. Studied. Staunch. Stern. Struggles. Strangled.

From time to time. That was quite a feat, he said. Whether or not. Without a second thought. Temporary. Tumescent. Triangular. Tonight.

On the march south . . . Originally there were six but now . . . Miles to go. Munitions to buy. Morning-glory. Monsters to slew. Mothers to love.

She came with arms outstretched & her hands . . . Overcome. Ocelot. Ostrich. Octagonal. Outboard. Overkill. Out of the dark.

Mark you this . . . Somewhere in back. Summersault. Salute. Sauté. Singular. Suspicion. Sonogram. Surreptitious.

From the basement . . . No one was left. After all these years. Nonsense. Nuance. Nincompoop. Niacin. Never again.

From what he'd read . . . Over the transom. Out of the box. Under the bed. Behind the barn. Between the sheets. A shovel of stars.

The one who initiates . . . Bubble-Gum. Broken Arrow. Eros. Hercules. Stagnation. Worrisome. Weather Man. Wonder Woman.

If only she had told him. What was her name? Who holds the cards? Quicksand. Sodomy. Singular. Hot-To-Trot. Enigma.

Name the final four Ports-Of-Call. Unwrap the sausage. Heat the pan.
Buttercup. Braggadocio. Berlin. Vanilla. Vacuum. Mumbly Peg.

If truth be known. Airtight. Aroma. Arsenic. Armageddon.
You're under arrest, she said. Fuck-You, he said. Mass Incarceration.

Moonscape. Monster movie. Minuscule. If & when . . . Helter Skelter.
Shoebox. Submarine. Open for me. However you want it.

Slumber Party. Sour Mash. Succumb. Birthday Cake. Binary. Blitz.
Orangutan. Oscar Wilde. Window Washer. Effortless.

Here comes the bride. Eruption. White & Withered. Worried & Weathered. It's you last chance. Tell it to the Judge. Crackerjack.

Beyond The Pale. Out for a run. Unperturbed. Neglect. Nowhere
to hide. Sunday. Soothing. Random. Toothache. Act of kindness.

Just suppose she . . . It's never that easy. Bottlebrush. Booby-trap. Bongos. Smorgasbord. Silhouette. Cantankerous. Sunlight &
Sabotage.

She never came home. Over the hill . . . He wouldn't take her back.
It's been a long time between sex & sanity. Mercy-Mercy-Mercy. Amen.

Roger Aplon

Spark

The concentration
Of certainty's particles.
You cannot rest,
Bathed, as it was,
In all that light

Next door
The floor boards
Peel backwards
In mock exaggeration
Of your terminal illness,
Trying to fill
The gaping holes
Desire for sanity cannot.

In Amsterdam
A hamster
Just Chewed its way
Through the cage door
Looking for its mate,
Sold separately from
The same pet store.

Love gets lost
In the shuffle
Self-assertion
Demands as it shatters
Any sense of wholeness,
Unlike a tree, which dances
Wildly and freely
From one firm place
In the deep secret of earth.

This Poem

the dog barks. the cats meow. the rain drops fall. it's sunday. venus and dante come visit. joanne is examining her still life. a blue bottle. a porcelain hand. a pine cone. wildflowers. why is the rabbit running? why do things drop when it is no longer raining? the world has gone crazy. drought and floods. drought and floods. a bird is buzzing on a high branch. a bird is buzzing on a high branch. throw her some food. throw her some food. joanne is petting the cats. their eyes big as stars. joanne is preparing her palette. a bird is chirping hello. joanne stares at the heart of her painting. moving across the day like a gazelle. pretending to be a fleet footed animal leaping across the landscape in search of the humming of refrigerators. the always open door. it sounds like a river here. on reynolds lane in shady new york. a river and a house. cats. dogs, rabbits. birds. paint. and this poem.

Bruce Weber

Shooting the Dog

He didn't have it in him.
He didn't have what it takes
to dig a hole

so he let the dog lay
where it fell:
a half-finished project;
a blemish on the landscape
as obvious as a fresh bruise
on his wife's face.

He grabs the bottle
by the handle, sinks it
into his mouth like a spade
into earth, floods his trenches
with muddy water & hope
that the memory will sink
into the silt & be lost
like some prehistoric mastodon.

Years later only the skull
remains: bone bleached
white by the Sun; a hole
as thick as a Bic pen
behind its left eye socket:

The self portrait of a man
with so many skeletons
in his closet he had to dump them
in the yard. It's funny, how

When the façade
of a visage is stripped
of its flesh, the skull smiles
loudly, like it knows

Flesh rots.
Bruises fade.
Bone Reminds.

He grabs the bottle
by the neck, hoping to choke
the air out of regret & he sinks
into the muddy water,
drowning; drowning out
that skull's last scream, the smack
of skin against skin; the stir
of the children to the crack
of the gun.

Mark Blackford

Still Looking

Again my eyes try holding back light,
again attempt to stop times' transit.

One heated noon, one summer, I watched
a snake cross the trail—night hunting light.

This was in the high lands, among our
world's oldest stones. All trees seemed

to turn away, bend to their own growth.
I stood before the dark seduction—

went on, as if I owned the right.
And I lost my way. Now, clouds plume

out of dawn's grasp, then gap. Now,
I look for the face of the god I wish

I knew. Not even a putti's foot.
What did I want that I didn't get, haven't got?

Blocked

Jim Eve

A starless June night
I take flight into dark
Looking for my muse.

Looking for my muse
I'm engaged In a process
Defined by chaos.

Defined by chaos
Thoughts run rampant...out of place
Avoiding paper.

Avoiding paper
Ink drips from suspended pen
In blotches...not words.

I sit quietly
Trying to capture thoughts
That want to run free...

I Think You Were In My Dream

I had a dream
I can't remember it
but I think you were in it

In this dream
someone asked me
why I hadn't graded
the stack of papers
that filled the room
from floor to ceiling

I think you were the person
who asked me

In this dream
when the Vikings raided
my village
and one of them stabbed
me through the heart
with an iron-tipped
wooden spear
and all the world
all of creation
all that ever was
and all that ever would be
began to drip black
and I felt my life
begin to ebb away
someone whispered in my ear
don't worry
this is only a dream
and you can never die
in your own dream

And I said
I thought it was
if you die in your dream
you die in real life

and as the blackness that started at
the edge
of my vision
obscured all there was
and all that there ever would be
this person whispered
in my ear
what idiot told you that?

I think that was you
who whispered in my ear

And
in my dream
I thrashed ecstatically in a tangle of
slightly frayed bedsheets
and entwined limbs and frantic kisses and smooth flesh
and fumbling caresses

I think that was you
tangled with me
in the slightly frayed bedsheets

I think that was you
I think you
were in my dream

Peter Ullian

Taking Out a Comma

> *"I was working on the proof of one of my poems all the morning and took out a comma…In the afternoon–well, I put it back again."*
> –Oscar Wilde

All morning I have been contemplating,
whether this comma belongs in or out,
and it seems to me that the devil does not care,
where commas go, or don't go.

Exclamation points? Well, that's another story!
I look on the exclamation point
as Satan hiding in the back room
ready to eat the spines of spiders,
or perhaps the gills of extinct fish
who swim only in the memory of the sea.
It seems so horrible to think of Satan
eating anything at all, let alone something
so priceless and irreplaceable!
But that's the devil for you! The more value
something has, the likelier he is to
destroy it. Look, after all, at the lovely,
mysterious connection between a warm man
and a warm woman. Boy, what a treat
for Satan to get between them
and inject a cold spell from the void
between galaxies!

Still, for finality, the exclamation point
must defer to the period, since
the exclamation point seems to point towards
something in the future, while the period says
that's all, folks! Imagine ghosts from
some ancient culture which
remains stubbornly unknown,
like the builders of Newgrange in Ireland,
known only for what they left behind
and the speculations of long-bearded professors
whose decades of study have left them with
highly-educated guesses worth their weight in
feathers, nothing you could publish in
The Saturday Evening Post, equally extinct.

She Says

A crazy woman
    lives in the attic.

She scribbles on walls,
scratches at the door.
    At night
    her room glows, though no light or candle burns.

She says
    it's the fire in her bowels she can't put out.

We worry
    the neighbors will notice, and then
the house is so hot and balmy,
smelling of her, we must open the windows.

When I go out I wear big hats.

She likes
    the blue velvet one best.
    It's soft she says.

She wants
    my hair loose and wild, like a
    lion's mane, and summer when clothing is skimpy
    so her skin can breathe.

She says she needs to breathe
    and complains about the compact car, the stuffy bedroom,
    ceilings, and the new housekeeper.

She says
    she's sure he's having an affair with her.

Last week she tore down
>	all the wallpaper and moved to the attic.

Now she's terrified of cellophane.
>	She resists bathing
>	and condoms—that slimy, taut latex chokes her.

>	"Someday
>	I'll bust through," she says,
>	>	"and burn this damned house down."

Reincarnation by Street Light

The strange behavior of street lights,
How they are magnetic to the eye.
When someone stands in their gaze,
    Illuminated as though by Heavenly Messenger,

Or when that light merely shines upon wet pavement.
And how they switch off when one approaches
    As if shy, as if to keep the night's secrets.
As if to let lovers steal kisses in private,
    To guard sorrows with darkness.

And I, fascinated by this device
    can only conclude:
In a previous life,
    I was a moth.

Against Dawn

In response to "Double Rape, Lynching in India Exposes Caste Fault Lines"
by Julie McCarthy

It's been said that for mangoes red does not mean ripe.
Why then did they take you from that tree, age 12,
only to tie you back to its branches? Torn
fruit cannot be returned by its stem to its root.
Didn't they squeeze gently and feel you were not ready?
Couldn't they judge by touch that your cousin was, too,
green at age 14—flesh pressing against thumbs in protest.
The aroma of womanhood had not yet infused the fields of your bodies.
In this place, mint, dung, and ash tour the nostrils,
casting a noxious concoction of sweet necrosis.
How you dangled there from fallopian branches,
paisley eggs fashionably sashed, swaying alongside leaves.
"And when they cannot control us, they kill us,"
a woman said. To be suspended by men
is the only way to reach their height:
a dream of weightless feet floating against dawn

Joann Deiudicibus

Marianna Boncek

Eleven and a Half Years

> *If we held one minute of silence for every victim of the Holocaust*
> *we would be silent for eleven and a half years.*

The first that would go
is the beep on the microwave.
We don't really need it anyway.
No one will miss the morning
alarm either.
It'll be nice to have no more
staff meetings
but the emails will increase exponentially.
The muted TV and the closed captions
might be a nighttime respite in your
overly noisy home.
It will take a while to teach
the babies not to cry
or the dogs not to bark.
Concert halls will close.
Musicians will take that long
awaited vacation.
Old ladies will be paid to carefully
sweep the road so the new noiseless cars
will not crunch the gravel.
Farmers will farm by hand, carefully,
and there will be no more sound
of the whirring combine.
Your mother will no longer call at an inconvenient time.
High heels will be packed away
As will be tap shoes.
Your lover will no longer sigh

or cry out your name.
Birds will fall silent.
You'll wear thick sweaters to muffle the sound
of your heart beating.
Tears will still fall because tears have always been silent.
But no one will laugh, not even giggle.
We will learn to speak with our eyes.

In the last minute
of the last day
of silence
someone will say, "May God comfort you
among all the mourners of Zion and Jerusalem."
And then,
"Arise."

We will hear the sound
of eight billion people
rising together.

Taking Flight

Dragonflies rise into the sky, a widening gyre,
vortex near my neighbor's stone fence
a bare place behind the cedars. I can wrap my arms
around the bottom as hundreds of dragonflies spiral
counter-clockwise. Reaching the top, twenty feet wide,
they fly off, but the spiral remains continuous.
No nymph hatch feeding the swirl, the forest gives birth.
A rift in matter's veil, dragonflies materialize
right out of the air.

Invitation from a nature spirit?
Step forward, exuviate your skin,
be sucked into the cyclone and transform, winged
illusion, iridescent fire whirling into a summer night.

I hold back. The spiral loosens,
the final few achieve the top at twilight. Scattering
to every direction, the dragonflies disappear
as birds fall silent and crickets take up the night watch.
I lumber home still in my skin, undress, crawl
into bed, close my eyes, intake then release
a breath; relax solar plexus,
dream in the speed of light.

Riverfront Green Park, Peekskill

Once I saw a single child
swinging alone from rung to rung
and a black-throated sparrow picking at a crust.
Behind, on an outcrop of the same flank,
two ribbed globes,
two blank boxes and an engineer's erection:
a herd of sullen beasts drinking of the grey river,
belching steam, shitting sludge
and gnawing at the bones of the Canada geese.
All the while, the faces of the cliffs,
charred and scarred, were turned away.

T. G. Vanini

Blue Balloon

Doing the Noah's Ark puzzle with a 4 year-old
whose parents crossed the border illegally makes me queasy.
Undocumented also means the species that wink out
before we write them down. The ones we don't notice.

The gathering clouds are effectively rendered in black crayon,
the lightning yellow zigzags suggest little time.
The familiar has packed a small red Paw Patrol backpack
and walked away.

I don't know what to tell this kid,
but this story's not doing it;
the animals will never line up in pairs
to walk the plank onto a boat made by humans.

And what are these dinosaurs doing in the puzzle?
We don't any of us understand time,
not to mention history and our place in it,
which is ultimately lonely.

Oh Vygotsky!, you said it is through others
that we know ourselves,
so I tell Jorge 'these are giraffes,
these are hippos, these are zebras'
as if securing both our futures.
But the wind keeps blowing harder in my backyard,
and it's clear that no one's in charge.

Yesterday I found a blue balloon in my daffodils
with a boy's name on it, Adam
an address 700 miles West,
its forest green yarn entwined
in yellow trumpets.

It must have felt its way blind
across the chasm between us,
bumbling like me,
its message of longing on folded paper
rattling away inside.

blot or the one percent

i saw his mouth curl up
the edge of a document in flames
and as his smirk crackled
smoke, at first from his ashen flesh,
then from behind closed doors,
continued to rise -
the promise of transparency a smokescreen
to blot out the solar plexus of the sun,
distract from the precipice,
the slick seas below.

but from this flame,
under a slow broth of blood and secrecy,
dark frogs begin to thrive:
shadow-songs of metamorphic rage.

new moon by new moon, ravens gather:
stewards of stories.
their primal power sits on my shoulder,
they perch on every tree, every cable, every post
the young test their wings, withstand
the wind – their voices clear.

one by one they lift off

fill the sky

a black

shimmering

scream.

december 5, 2010

Marina Mati

The House

The house was not the same anymore after fall, after the leaves changed color and fell. It was not the same after they'd emptied out the closets, hung curtains straight from their plastic. The house was not

it's smell, the must of it, the creak in the stairs. The house was not where she had perched to hear her brother's tempered breathing on the last step from the top, to check for life. That breath wasn't there anymore and her memory puts her further and further from the source:

open scaling, pulling out taffeta from trunks, the source of the memory. The smell of it thick like oak and paper left too long in the sun. How kind to forget the heft of it, the terrible churn of the house, how it stood or stands like an echo & inside - her

in all those rooms. Baited hands spreading notebooks on the tile floor, smoothing down the pages, praying that way for release. The house was full of doors. Not all the doors locked. She found spaces there to tether together how a childhood looks: sequined and oxidized, belligerent in its silences,

cold, hard and begging to crack open. Ask me where to go now, how to tell the story, where the leaves go, how the color's lost or when he cut it down how the body laid in the yard for years, grew its own botany, reached up again for the sun from the rot in itself. That's how you tell the story of the house. You are the house, you're buried

with it - totemic, infinite - and then you claw out from the ground, take the creaking with you and make it sing. Those holed places you've cut into yourself don't get filled, but weep for the space they've created in you. And say you're sorry and thank you and tell the story from that rotted space you grow out of. Tear the house down, build a new one. Let the new one sing of the old one, how it cataracted you and laced itself into gauzy visions you could not wake up from. Bear witness to the foundation, the plasterboard of your knees and elbows, the chipped shingling of your breath. Ask all the questions, open all the kitchen cabinets, use every last cup and plate until the taste

of the house tells its own story on your tongue. Because the house is not the same anymore, you are not in it - carry the light of that around in your palm, on your eyelids. It is a gift.

Irene O'Garden

Sergeant Eleanor Is Laid To Rest
In Which a Bird Appears.

                (Note: I call the words and phrases in superscript "fulcrums."
                When the poem is read aloud, the fulcrums are read twice.)

Sergeant Eleanor is laid to rest
in fields of blooming [yellow mustard] eggs
in silver buckets later at the salad [bar] thoughts
of army [women] in the service Sergeant
Eleanor was happy. Fought for freedom
and was [happy] giving and receiving [orders]
of nuns almost [army women in the forties] served
a god-shaped [army] in peacetime
couldn't use this [soldier] on did

Sergeant Eleanor: [husband, baby]. Twice.
Third man no better. No matter.
A daughter. A son. Lives to guard, [honor]
Sergeant Eleanor, who [fought for freedom]
when divorce drew fierce artillery
of [shame] as well in purplehearted sacrifice
of factory [work] of loneliness like flaying
[bayonets] stripped from barrels by the honor guard
at her [grave] looks on the veterans; warring

Sergeant Eleanor wore costume jewelry,
turquoise and magenta, [fought on] vodka,
cigarettes, bedtime stories, in combat
with doctors, bankers, teachers.
For these kids. That clear? Motherhood:
a hundred thousand acts of bravery
and a helluva lemon meringue.

Sergeant Eleanor ^(made herself) goddam heard.
Three shots shock like broken eggs' ^(shells) fly
from ^(soldiers' rifles) lay a soldier
in the ^(grave) salute flag ^(folded) wings

Sergeant Eleanor's daughter and son
open the car ^(at the crossroads of dust) shrieks
from a rust-ringed feathered throat
Kildeer at the right front tire,
        fatherless ^(her dusty nest) a gravel patch.
Two speckled ^(eggs) warm with life.

Irene O'Garden

Coffee Break

Before Philip Seymour Hoffman was world-renowned as an actor, he was just Phil.

In 1990, we were both young actors trying to get a break in New York City, so sharing mutual friends granted us countless opportunities to glare at each other from across the room, sizing each other up, competition between two young egos. In the meantime, while waiting for the gods of show-business to bequeath us a shot at fame, we worked menial jobs in-between auditions.

It's December in Manhattan, Gramercy Park, Sunday, mid-afternoon. I jauntily stride in to an upscale corner Italian deli for a cup of coffee. I have cash in my pocket and I'm wearing my long blue woolen coat that I scored from the second-hand store (before they were called vintage boutiques). I wear my collar pulled up and think I look like James Dean. The door slams shut behind me and the little bell jingles alerting the help that a customer has arrived. I peruse the shop, sizing-up danishes and cream filled pastries, taking my time, enjoying the luxury of my imagined lavish wealth and success, pretending I'm the actor about town waiting for the curtain to rise. I notice an employee straightening stuff up, doing what employees do in places like that; polishing a coffee urn, refilling the cream, replenishing the sugar, and I spy Phil. He's wearing a white apron and standing behind the counter. I quickly avert my gaze. From the corner of my eye I can see him spot me. I catch his reflection in the window and I can see his head drop and his body cave-in a little. I don't want to embarrass him so I keep my back turned and fake interest in a muffin display, giving him a moment to puff himself back up. When I turn around, he's gone. He's taken his break. I can get coffee now. I approach the counter and consider an espresso with lemon. I can't handle the brew but pretend I'm sophisticated and order a double. Behind the counter is the kitchen and behind the kitchen is a door leading to the outside garbage area, it's wide open and I can see Phil having a smoke.

He's escaped the humiliation of having to serve another actor a cup of .75 cent coffee. Little does Phil know that I'm just minutes off my shift from being an apartment cleaner. Phil wears an apron during his shift. I wear Playtex gloves during mine. I had 60 dollars in my pocket from cleaning a two bedroom, two-bathroom apartment. That means I scrubbed two toilets, at least one bathtub, scoured an oven, wiped-clean a refrigerator, mopped a kitchen floor, vacuumed, dusted, did the dishes, and Phil was embarrassed to serve me coffee. I downed my cup and spun out of there dizzy with caffeinated enthusiasm ready to embrace the day, and somehow, feeling a little ashamed.

It was not long thereafter that any competition which may have existed between Phil and I, imagined or otherwise, was quickly eradicated by his brisk departure from a life of servitude to his rapid ascension into fame, and as I, just as rapidly, descended further into obscurity and a continued life of servitude for some time. Years later, in a movie magazine, I read Phil's account of being rescued from working in a coffee shop by getting an acting job in a movie called Scent of a Woman. I read that article during my coffee break, just before I returned to cleaning another toilet.

Michael Sean Collins

Vicious Ending

On a cold February Morning
 outside the New York City Courthouse.

Released into the care of the Mother that birthed
 and enabled my Demons – and the Horse
on which I can ride off into Eternal Night.

I can't remember if I killed her
 and I'm not sure which was worse:
Withdrawing on the cold hard prison floor
 or the pain, of what's not known,
For 5 months building like anticipation of that first dope sick hit
     then suddenly
 The party ends.

Only 2 Hours passed since revived from a blue lipped oblivion
 and asking for more – I can't do this on my own. Mother, please
Fill my veins with the only love I have left in this life.
Help me to end the suffering – Bury me in Leather

I want to go be with Nancy.

First Day of Autumn

It's nice to feel an air conditioned day,
Nature's changing thermostat
set just where I like.
Leaves on the trees disagree:
some are red with anger
that Mother Nature turned off the heat,
some are yellow with fear
for the coming chill of winter,
and some have fainted dead away,
lying on the ground.

Corrected Versions

Lately, while I climb I pause to see
    the flame in hand, what it illuminates—you,
        all of you—
who scramble, fall, in shadows all around.
It feels like wisdom to notice you, the light,
    my bloody fingers, the scraped walls.

I make the same old mistakes.
Not even her death, or all the deaths,
    keep me from error.
Every moment of fire is new flame
    newer than thought, newer than brain's delay.

Eye is tardy, or jump-ahead.
All we have is the unending memory of fire, just now—
    we stare but never catch up or get ahead—
    to where heat lives, light resides.
To the tragic, microscopic moment of combustion.

Flame is a reminder: we are not really here.
It is all memory and anticipation.
She was here, but now
    she was never really here...
Every moment of life is
    burdened by thought, by brain re-runnery
Eye's tardy inattention, the unending
    itch for what's next, what was.

We suck. We don't *really* see, not ever.
We press up against the next moment,
    dragging our descriptions,
        the returns on investments of
            old observations, old pretenses
                of paying attention...

We cower behind corrected versions,
    afraid to go forward into what we say we want,
    what we endlessly describe to ourselves:
        this is what it will be...
        this is what I'll have...
    afraid to know the ones we say we know
    and endlessly describe to ourselves:
        this is who she was...
        this is how she looked...

What we have is the dark well below
    pulling us down, insisting.
What we have is the fable of
    blue perfection, high overhead.

We pretend to rise while we climb.
All we do is scramble in shafts, peering below, afraid—
    what was *was not* what it was,
        we never really knew her—
    or we stare straight up, possessed by visions, afraid—
        heaven *pretends* to be heaven
        but is just terror—always was—
        colored Sky Blue Sky Blue Sky Blue...

There will be no reclamation
    of all the moments we would not see.
No reconciliation with the ones we lost
    before they were lost.
We will never catch the flame being flame.
All we have is the darkness below.
    The holding, and not letting go,
        in a guttering light.

Greg Correll

Cabbage

What fine reserve, o cabbage,
tight leaves folded round
to form such a confident sphere!
So modest in your price per pound!
Your tone a light and floating green
like the squid's dream of a drawing room.
Your gravity and earnestness
evident in the warning
of your fibrous snap
which unapologetically declares,
"I expect too much neither of myself
nor of you." How comfortable a thought!
Yet there you are: a few sharp bits by a taco,
translucent and visionary
when stuffed and baked,
or simply sitting on the table,
a swollen solid pale and glorious ball.

The April Showers Gate

Through the Gate , raffia adorned,
She rests beside an Anglican Dream,
And then speaks to me in Gaelic song .
Follow the black squirrel, to the fiery terra-cotta hue .
Mulch and hay for grass blades , finally, to a peek - a - boo .
I know the words in the poem "We Do Not Die",
Today, I'll promise not to cry .
Then come a vision , the Phoenix in my head .
As I place white flowers on driftwood, bind ,
Berries of tinted rose , and thyme .
Wet with mist, no restraint - I come to spiritual bliss.
In synchronicity, fell a tree behind.

Sharon Ferrante

Henri Rousseau Answers Questions

Because the white lake of canvas waits for me.
The lovely free space invites me to wander,
to arrive at some unforeseen destination.

No, I was never afraid of the distance
where France vanishes.
Did I say how grateful I am?
                              Believe me,
I know all about Hamlet's nutshell – here,
I am king of a thousand leaves, animal eyes,
the bewildering body,

and my garden blooms without withering
and my garden overruns its borders
and my garden swells to the sea

where I skim the tender
curve of this blue world in the bright
boat I have fashioned. Look

at what falls into shadow, into
a hundred shades of green,
the splay of leaf and blossom

where person and panther connive,
where the tiger holds a deer-like creature
in its teeth, stilled in a frozen paradise.

You say I've made the savage and the exotic
curiously tame? Yes, the ripping of flesh is silent here
and the lion could almost lie down with the lamb.

The Sunflower

For: Jennifer Juneau & Thomas Walker

A camera caught it
growing in a dim lit crowded bar's
smoky atmosphere no more
or less real than what
was taking shape that
cold January night
a woman with long blond hair
looking up at a man
whose arms frame what
is blooming in her gaze slowly
overtaking everything else:
there was nothing else

Solitaire

My father didn't read like the rest of us;
hour after hour he played Solitaire,
dealing through the deck again and again
by immutable rules, toward the strange end
of "winning" at the game. We knew he was home
when we heard the rapping of the deck
as he straightened the cards for shuffling.
Isolated, pointless, it was like his life.

The British grant virtue to the game by calling it
Patience, no reward except completion
of the pattern, skill useful but less important
than the luck of the shuffle—whatever happens,
you can blame the cards—and thus a paradigm
of existence. Sometimes when I should work,
I sink in addiction to the computerized game,
moving the mouse till my arm aches.

I try to control myself, to keep from clicking
the Solitaire icon, which will summon up
the cards, crisply pictured, almost real,
waiting for clicks to reveal what's hidden.
W. H. Auden asked T. S. Eliot
why he played Patience so much.
Because, said Eliot, *it's the nearest thing*
to being dead.

Evasion

Determined
by crush
    of water, un-
avoidable col-
lision. In-
evitable wreck.

By this am
I haunted.
Last one in. Last one
out.

 Delusion, collusion-
marriage - that
necessary
    torque.

 I had been headed
for disaster
    anyway,
crumpling up
tissues into
roses
the way I did.

A wreck is
a wreck
is a wreck,
as secret as
the place
I hid. You
too take
shelter.
You be
warned.

Ruth Danon

Spellbound

Spellbound. Words escape me. Going out
as if a flame. Extinguished. My capacity
to want anything

In this transport the temperature is dropping
on the top floor of the walk up. The mane
of a nameless horse. Tossed back
among the waves in your eyes. The blue heaven
and the open sea bringing the sundered night
to an end. In the web of separate things
the flight of the night's lost bird is ending
on the most remote corner of the world
an explosion in me. Lying in the ashes
of a dress. My ember wings make a last
fluttering gasp knowing they've seen
enough. Downstairs
the linoleum is covered with a carpet
of bleeding prayers and the walls and ceiling
take on its glow. No other hand but yours
reaches out of the sky-drifts
to check the fire. No other hand

Spellbound. Words escape me. Going out
as if a flame. Extinguished. My capacity
to want anything

In this transport the temperature is dropping
in a cold ray of moonlight
on your bed
I pass away
annihilated
from head to foot
in the fortress
of your aloneness

At Any Given...

At Any given longitude   a banner of wind   Beethoven's *Ode to Joy* unfurled
in mid ocean   stars etched sails on my breast plate   gazing north in late winter
I mounted Taurus   & held the faceted crystal fingers   of the Gemini twins
without distinction between sky & sea   to cling to life   I gripped the railing

In mid ocean   stars etched sails on my breast plate   gazing north in late winter
you never escaped the sound of the waves   racing through the constellations
without distinction between sky & sea   to cling to life   I gripped the railing
one evening the Captain invited us into his wood & windowed observatory

You never escaped the sound of the waves   racing through the constellations
the Zvir was equipped for electronic navigation   but celestial guidance was fixed
one evening the Captain invited us into his wood & windowed observatory
very old school   as every mariner is in love   with the bright alert of Polaris

The Zvir was equipped for electronic navigation   but celestial guidance was fixed
compass   quadrant & sextant   he kept the tools of his student days   at hand
very old school   as every mariner   is in love   with the bright alert of Polaris
at any given longitude   a banner of wind   Beethoven's *Ode to Joy* unfurled

Janet Hamill

Catskill Thunder

Each thunder storm this year gave
Way to clarification.
Lightning has various shades of
Color.
While thunder has a variety of voice
From roaring lion to metal sword
Clashings against forgotten warriors.
Heavy downpours of rain that slides
Or dots the ground with balls of
Hardened ice.
The Catskills are the tropics of the
North East.
Even Rip Van Winkle's elfin dwarves
Could hinder no game as loud
                            as fierce.
Mother Nature on menopause or
Earth changes abound.
Thunder in the distance is like an
Ired woman during orgasm

Trevor and the Pterodactyl

Wild turkeys amble through our yard
    like pterodactyls, their piston-like haunches
jut heads forward with each step.

Every spring these dinosaurs fan their tails
    for strutting season, to impress
their conquest, prove they're not ugly

like their vulture-cousins, but majestic
    and gentle. Last year one lingered
behind, content to wander alone scratching

for grubs and new grasses. Trevor the Terrible,
    our resident coyote, emerged from the bush
and loped across the lawn. The Tom froze,

elongating his neck till it looked as though
    it would snap, his bald head flushing pink.
but Trevor the Terrible only gave him

a casual glance and kept roving except
    for a short pause to scratch an itch.
Our turkey slowly went back to mine for roots

and bugs. Two days later, feathers
    scattered the yard,
only one wing left

This Country Could Break My Heart

Slicked back hair, tooled boots,
ten-gallon hat that makes the head seem big.

Broad hands, callused, quick to clench
those women always running into fists.

*Blood's easier than love, love's short,
somebody's gonna cheat and break my heart,*

this country says. *Oh lonesome road
I can't resist, outside the law's not cold*

*but free. Ain't nobody can challenge me
without a fight,* this country says.

Those old vows, hard to make, prove
harder still to keep. A roving

eye, that's what this country has,
and jealous heart. And sweet talk

that could melt the Arctic ice. And does.
Draws toxic rush deep in the lungs

and blows out perfect smoke rings
that could wreathe

the worst defeat. On borrowed cash
stands on its own two feet.
Sticks up for friends, that's what
this country does, even the one

that lie and steal and cheat.
And never met a man it didn't like,

and never met a man it couldn't kill,
and has a most prodigious appetite.

But when that song comes whistling
down the lane, that familiar step clanks

on the porch, I curse us both before I hear
the rap, unlatch the triple-bolted door again.

Variations on a Line from The New York Times

Across the river, lifeblood of their countries,
    soldiers were shooting.
A river divides the countries.
Soldiers were shooting the river.
The river shoots between two countries.
Soldiers shoot each other across the river.
Two countries divide the river.
Each soldier tries to shoot his country
    across the river.
The countries divide the soldiers
with the river. Two countries shoot
the soldiers. Why does a river divide
the soldiers? How do countries divide
a river? Blood tributaries merging in the river
    that divides their countries

From the author's book World Enough, and Time (Kelsay, 2017)
originally published in Waymark

Between Daylight And The Deep

All's quiet, like this morning,
when you left without a salutation.
Haloed by a reading lamp, you seem

oblivious to the settling dusk,
my entrance just another piece of pattern
now familiar, nine years into marriage.

What can I share from my day
and what let settle into gathering shadows?
The cards, the trinkets from co-workers,

their buzz 'round my 30th birthday lunch?
You'd like their choice of Japanese -
food graciously prepared at table.

But what about the "Glory" roses Tom brought:
pink tinged with gold, mild scent of mango,
flaming the glow on my cheeks?

The roses emblazon as the highlight of my day.
But let silence surround the flowers, here,
while I prepare to meet

no devil, no deep blue sea,
only a deepening twilight
between work and dinner in the dark.

The Rub
a golden shovel

> *If you are irritated by every rub*
> *How will your mirror be polished?*
> —Rumi

Reflection is overrated. You wonder if
I speak of thought or shiny surfaces. You
Should know I set no store by salves that are
meant to save us; skin stretched taut, irritated
from lotions, perfumes, unctions, ointments by
which we becloud ourselves, lashed to every
masque in which we revel. Take some alcohol and rub
your complexity clean. If not for lack of thinking, how
will you see yourself to sleep? If not for lack of light, how will
you suckle darkness? Have you passed the middle of your
life? Your features slide like molten silver in the dusky mirror.
You clasp the chain around your wrinkled neck. The bee
ignores the wilted flower. Your chest of days needs polished.

Susan Chute

Sepia Life

He cited Catholic heresy,
claimed the city was trying
to divorce him,

it was winter, their relationship
down to bedrock, his face the color
of gothic towers, of pylons sunk
in the East River, the cement
he sometimes slept on.

Knew where all the great writers
had lived: Willa Cather, Bank Street,
e e cummings, Christopher Street.
John Cheever, Jane Street.

Air honed with frigidity,
the nearest shelters shut
for the night: the Bowery,
Lafayette, East 4th.

 On East 4th, Hunter Thompson.
Ginsburg and Burroughs, East 7th.

Steam rises through the teeth
of the steel grates, he can feel
the pressure beneath his feet,
the sidewalks arcing up, ready
to blow, the streetlights eating
their own illumination.
Steinbeck, Salinger, Capote.

His mother and her tight smile,
laid up in bed away from
the light, her body like a prop.

Eugene O'Neill, born in the
Barrett Hotel, 43rd and Broadway.
Tennessee Williams, found dead
in his suite at the Hotel Elysee,
East 54th.

The snow is sweeping in
from Jersey, white silk over all
the restlessness, over the currents
of the Hudson, the waters of the Sound,
Melville, Hemingway, Kerouac,
the deep recess of a doorway
on Spring Street, pulling all he owns
about him.
      From the loft above
music muscles through brick
and glass, through the drowning
wind, the fist of his voice, body
singing, mind caught upon time.

Home

Childhood in a tract house:
eight feet of earth marking
the boundary between neighbors,
springing green for two weeks
every April
before dying back to the color of a tin can.
Each family claiming half and laying in
slabs of colored flagstone
or cunningly uneven shapes of shale,
the better to catch the feet of children
and send them laughing toward five more stitches.
And the dog won't shut up—
you'd think it'd never licked
blood before,
like raw hamburger had never been tossed its way
from the incessant weekend barbecue—
everyone fired up on Saturday, lighter fluid
and a six pack of Schaeffer mixed into a 1950's cocktail
that just doesn't taste the same
all these years later.
You blame the brewery for changing the formula,
you blame the farmers for impure hops,
and you blame God for allowing acid rain
to spoil the fermenting process.
Because all you're trying to do is
pull back a jag of memory sharp as
the chipped lip on a long-neck bottle,
the one your father snuck you so
you could taste what it was like
to be an adult.
And when your lip bloodied from the drinking,
it didn't really matter which house you turned to.
You could have called any one of them
home.

Catalogue

Composition— He said, "At the desk every morning, Monday through Friday. Take the weekends off."

Industry— children raised on a schedule

Memory— cast back over water that remembers a bridge

Justice— a test of refractive in(tro)spection

Downtime—just wait a minute

Cellphone—all my friends here with me now

Subway— living dead space in time

Camaraderie— sit and listen

Sidewalk— men young bursting reckless

The family— walk through a series of spirals

Bookstore— miles of titles on spines

History— cells accumulated sloughing off

Explaining His Craft— discursive, slow in what was the question acted upon when

Music in childhood— sound from the parents' side of the wall

Faithfulness— lost and found

Representation— in place of;taking the place of;taking place away from;replaced in the land of;place-taken;taken away

A friend dies— close his eyes

Ambition— howling alone or in public

THE ROMANTIC HERO— all in capitals

Nude on the wall— ink-washed breasts

How to greet an acquaintance after many years— cheeks passing one quarter to one half-inch apart wisps of hair light or dark

Ambiguity— generosity

Generosity— forgetful

Father

My hair go aflame
as he hiccups and breathes the last of this earth.

A gray wart appears on my forehead.

I clasp your cold palms
to feel blackout of your blood vessels.

On your chest I burst
a silent pitcher of my life's sleep

Darkness,
a savage silence of Sunya's eternal ocean.

I glisten your rubbery body
from honey, curd and milk of seven rivers;

a tear keeps rolling endlessly
on the naked wound of my secret grief.

For the last time I hold
this face of yours in my trembling hands;

blast of a wail
ravages sunlight of my faith.

On your body I place
heavy logs damp from a history of vanquished hearts.

In the crack of your still mouth
I drop grain of a rainbow
and light the last fire
that shall blacken quiet pages of my youth.

I hit the center of your skull
aflame in the spluttering pyre

to ignite a bejeweled passage to eternity.

On the flooded banks of the Ganges
I knead your limbs all over again;

I make your head
heart, hands, life-veins, lines of your fate.

From the mantras of my breaths
I feed hunger of your blood vessels

and see you go alone
along the blazing fields of The Garuda Purana

eating crumbs of the blessed food
lost in the memories of my childhood

when once you has lifted me
up in the fragrant stretch of the blue hillside air

and probably for the first time
in your life, smiled...

November, so we leave nothing but the bones

They'd placed them in rows along the windowsill just like you'd set pieces of hard candy or buttons and bottle caps or perhaps acorns—tiny objects that take up tiny spaces. Where only the light was sure to meet up with them. My grandfather holding me up to take a look at them in the frosty brightness. The smokehouse in winter. And the eyes of a deer in my pocket.

Hirundo Rustica

It was the easiest thing in the world to do. They sat there on the wire so perfectly still that it was hard to believe these were the same creatures that came diving out of the air, swooping past your head and into the barn where their muddy nests clung to the beams like cow dung. It gave me the creeps how still they were, like hanging bats isolated in their interior world. So withdrawn were they that you could imagine reaching out and picking them up in your bare hands. That's what repulsed me—their vulnerability in this moment of resting on the wire. In these static, frozen moments—like the dead in coffins up close. What were they thinking just now as I carefully extended the rifle out the barn window and laid the sites onto their barely breathing breasts.

I got my ass beat on two accounts. One for the dead swallow my old man found in the grass outside the hog pens with a pellet in its breast. And two for the bent sites on my great-grandfather's antique pellet rifle. I told him it slipped out of my hands as I climbed into the haymow. But that didn't keep his belt off my ass. At least in the end I knew where I'd sent that swallow—somewhere so far away not even my dad could get there, not yet.

Half Assed Pegasus

Since my car will run on neither oxygen nor electricity
I've got to stop at the local Mobil to get some poison.
Maybe it's because of the cold wind and rain
but I find my head slanted down towards the ground.

And on the pump in front of me
there it is
flat and red
same as I've been gazing at
since I was 3 feet tall.
Half Assed Pegasus

Even the child of me knew there was something big
about this unfriendly but winged horse
and here I stand now
all these years later
gazing at this little crystallization
of myth and the unconscious
adorning not a temple,
but my local pump.

A strange feeling of unwarranted continuity
flows over me, as the gas flows into my car.
And I notice how rudimentary this Pegasus is.
Seems it only has to be good enough to invoke the mythic
'cause this thing looks like it was done with a stencil.

Now that I think about it
seems like some kind of crime of the soul
falsely linking something from the realm of infinity

to a product for commercial gain.
And then working that association
working it for my whole life.

From now on
every time I see that shameless appropriation
I'm going to think of the little boy who saw it and wondered
if there could really be a horse with wings.
And I'm going to tell him to look elsewhere for his wonder
and to remind him that this great archetype
has been painted and written about by great artists
throughout the centuries.

As a matter of fact, next time I'm able
I might just get me an electric car.

Walking My Dog During a Florida Thunderstorm

The rainclouds appear as a puffy silk shelf
from which gray garland cotton balls hang
from the swollen sky
like ribbons of Christmas ornaments.

Cracks of thunder crackle with
streaks of lightning that explode,
light up the darkness in flames
like oil and water sizzling in a frying pan.

A spectacle of spears
slice the heavens
illuminate the water-logged particles,
like dancing minstrels parading the engorged highway.

All this,
while my dog pissed and shat.

Dennis Wayne Bressack

My Friend Che

Who wouldn't want to be friends
With Che Guevara?
I'm earnest for my Ernesto,
Got a Mat Damon for my Ramon,
I'm gay for Che,
Hot as Sahara for Guevara.

And oh,
Did his United Fruit
Limber up from his crotch hirsute
Spraying his jubilee juice
Into Sancti Spiritus?

Who wouldn't want to make love
With Che Guevara?
And toke on that sweetly fumin' cigarro
From this bloke of a sweetly human cigarerra?

Want to take him to my villa
Or to a new kind of
Thrilla in Manilla
Where this Argentine guerilla
In Cuban garb
Can throb his knob like a shish-kebab
And transform my Gringo lingo
Into a lingua franca from far Sri Lanka
As I flap like a queer flamingo
While he Jaggers my Bianca.

Who *wouldn't* Fidel and Raoul
In a ghoul's super drool
For the cool, cool, tool
Of Che Guevara?

Got Caught Up In Out

here's a story:

I once dressed as a man, became the sum of my parts with a wig,
became a left-handed tremor, settled along sky's indiscriminate veins,
seeked new tools, became a boy, bared my brain, peeled a cave,
became a secret, doily pants and cigars in my rectum, found space
by standing, became a jester for vessels, cracked open what I could
never hold, became a pair of hands for God, lit fuses with halitosis,
strangled farts with each knuckle, became liquidy spine along
naked back, searched for the bobble from crux to cortex, became a page
for a heart, took a corner from purity, yawned into history's face
and burned off mine, became a smokescreen, found pleasure in the
frictive,
drifted over stammer, taking each punch, became a dance for sacrilege,
tears for trying, settled on a kiss before I was ready, became a collision
searching for a crash, explosive where I can't look now, became a girl
with umbilical pants, wearing a dictionary for a jockstrap, murmured
to my mantra, you've done it too, became a human ear, traveled deep,
inverted folding skin, dripped delicate darlings on aroma's areola,
revered by reverie, became sleepless stigmata, tired in the reach,
itched where I shouldn't, looked behind me, marveled at the glow
of what surrounds, became firewater, drank myself, burped silent air,
became a man again, how boring, became a boy again, quickly,
became a knuckle, and then its yawn, became a dance again,
a rock, a stone, a rooster, a punch, a pool of defending
decisions, became a tremor one more time, wondering how quick
to leave something, before it wants what it becomes

Love Jones

Unspecified time and place
Not an anticipated act of choice
But yeah! An orgasm of feeling
Irresistible urge that smothers everything except itself
Makes you want to weep and sing sad songs:
(Ain't no sunshine when she's gone")
Nothing matters when she's near
The closest thing to holy here on earth,
      wholeness drug addictive and lasting
A onetime ride on the fulfillment train,
        an express with tracks laid floating on a cloud.

Dream The Night John Lennon Was Shot

You know what—I didn't have any cause
you know what I was doing? I was trying
to get over on some fat-ankled New England
MBA with corn yellow hair and a name
off the Mayflower manifest and we walked
from one bar to another trying to outrun
the news and I could tell she had little
to no connection to the murder beyond

the fact that it was a goddamn shame, because
what did John Lennon ever give her?
She was nine when the Beatles split, her songs
were Genesis and fucking Kiss—Kiss!
I could hardly swallow my tequila.
Cause you know what my connection was?
You know what John Lennon gave to me?
He gave me my haircut, my sneer, my boots,

my voice, my hats, my hope, my joy, my guts,
my ticket to ride, my nuts, my mind games,
my broken goddamn heart, the blisters on
my fingers, and songs I've sung a thousand
times and some of those I'm still trying to
figure out and what did the Mayflower MBA
give me? A handjob, a handkerchief,
a hangover, and a copy of the Marx-Engels Reader

she wouldn't be needing when she moved
into banking. Morning, December 9,
walking north on Broadway when everyone else
streamed south, thinking ... I'm a loser
and I lost someone who was near to me,
look at me, look at me goddamnit, I've
got something to hide. I think a no but
I mean a yes, but it's my pride yes it is,

yes it is, oh yes it is ... and here am I sitting
all on my own, two foot small, goo goo g-joob.

Tim Tomlinson

A Poem About Our Fuck Last Wednesday

before Psychophysics II, which you knew
I hated, was, in fact, failing, in part
because the professor was a grinning
con-man whose TAs polished his wing-tips,

but at least as much because I could not
get you out of my mind every breathing
second of every bleeding class, even
the ones I supposedly liked: "Joyce, Pound,

and Eliot," "Fellini, Bergman, Freud,"
French II with that hot young adjunct from Egypt.
And there we were, in late afternoon sunlight,
on your desk—your desk!, with the notebooks

and the ash trays and the Our Bodies,
Ourselves crashing to the floor around us.

Death Is A White Catfish

Death is, a white catfish
With a small strip of red on it's mouth
from the hook ripped out.

Seen so clearly through a blue smoke cloak of war,
Embroidered, by the white bones of men.
It is also the small wooden bat that the young fisherman smash down
        on the fish head before they throw it laughing, back into
        the scar of a brown river.

The hate and fear filled words whispered
that set the event in motion.
It can be a gourmet, served in large dinners and luxurious supple
        women wrapped in white embroidered silk kimono
        smelling of peonies.

But in the morning dark nipples are always white,
always a pointed painted fin.
A spiked drop of blood in your urine.
A Pain in the soft parts.
What could be stranger than being born?
She asked just before she stopped breathing.

You, you keep casting your line into the brown slash moving passed
You, always wondering what the mouths of sun opening and closing
        reflecting golden from the surface are asking us

Oh no God. Oh God no!

Secrets abound on the correct bait to bring this leviathan.
The perfect triangulation of recipe for catching death.
The monks tell us, Just wait, have faith.

As you peer dizzy into the darker dark of the moving mass of slag
        looking for it's white eye.
Have faith, they say it will find you.

Shotsie Gorman

The Whole Crowd

Renaissance popes
Anarchists
American history
History of Burma
The age of the stream
Steam
The Atlantic City diving horse
Plastic in their bellies
Traders on the beach
And in the bars
A flush beats a straight
Every day and always
Those ways.
They were there for the blitz.
Oh the northern lights.
Oh the sun.
Oh animals who burrow.
The Medici were not so nice
But neither are Blue Jays.
Is anyone left alive ?
Such a question.
Ice skating with the Easter Bunny.
A Confederate flag flutters nearby

Happy As A Lark?

Did you ever see a lark,
Or a love-of-your-life,
Or dew on eagles' wings,
Wafting through the air?

I was up with the lark this morning
And I am happy as a lark.
A song wafting though very thin air .

When to have and to hold
Was a real estate term
For sullen Republicans

And bad music
Frogmarched us
Into happiness

As vacant as the ethos
Of a mollusk
In a damp time

While Shakespeare's lark,
The break-of-day lark,
Stayed down on sullen ground

And could not sing
At heaven's gate
Nor be as happy as a clam

Fred Poole

A Catholic Girlhood in Queens

Her life was:
Frank Sinatra on the radio
Hiding cigarettes
In the top of her uniform
Going to bars on Saturday night
With her daddy
And bowling at the Legion Post
On Sunday.

"You broke your Father's heart!"
I shout at her.
"You won't break mine!"

She turns slowly away
Already becoming someone else
And tucks her soul
Behind a barrier unbroken.

Breasts

Among the cruel jokes between us,
as lovers have, slipping back and forth
between the lands of adoration and distaste,
are ones about my unused breasts.

They've spent their lives as intensive magnets
set to test the young men of my early school years,
nicknames like "Twin Towers," meant to
laugh away their fascination.

Perhaps they were adored in silence then, too,
the star in someone's late, afterschool
masturbation melodrama,
me and my real flesh safely out of sight.

They've been toys, too,
good for warm-up to
brief encounters, and longer interludes,
spanked and kneaded as
older playmates explored their
potential, pale pots of
Silly Putty, warm globes of iridescence
at their momentary disposal.

Biological function never fulfilled,
we joke now about the dust collecting
where milk ducts are supposed to be.
We imagine great, sweet clouds emerging at the
slightest squeeze, like dandelions caressing their young.

There is no flavor in me
that would have satisfied an infant's hunger,
no untapped craving to sustain another life.
From the time I weaned myself,
my breasts were never here to nurse the world.

I suckled myself, completing a circuit of need,
reliance, self-made woman.

Marta Szabo

The Visit

He has come for a visit
Flying in from Hungary
Where he lives now because he can't afford the States.

My father.
So fragile I must take care of him.
Not his health. That's fine.
Everything else.

When I introduce him to a girlfriend my father explains that
He commutes between Hungary and the States.

My inner eye rolls.
You aren't commuting.
You wish you were commuting
Wish for that luxury
That elegance
That ability to impress.

Instead, my mother –
Who works odd jobs through the Pennysaver –
Paid for your ticket and you stayed with her
And now with me.

Standing in a corridor
You bring from a pocket
A digital device,
Black plastic, battery run,
An instrument to track addresses or appointments.
It looks like a calculator.

You want to show me how it works.
I don't want to even look at it.
Dad, that little instrument is not cool
Or futuristic.
It looks cheap and third world
And the sight of you holding it
With some kind of pride
Breaks my heart and makes me furious.

But you aren't really so fragile.
As you prepare to leave the room where you have stayed a week
You sit in the corner armchair and smiling insist
I open every drawer
Search the under-bed floor
For what you may
Have left behind.
And I do it,
Breathing fury
On hands and knees.

The Nieves Flores Library, Guam

They cut the funding for the Library.
Its outside walls bleed black tropical fungus
No money to water blast and paint
It's become a mind slum.

Schoolgirls come there only to pretty eye acne'd boys
Pretending to homework, but really
Posing peacock in early mating games.
Libraries are ordained to be elegant in their Tinkerbell'd dust
But this one has been rusted out and abandoned,
As if its walls had been shelled in some subtle war
A gaping hole open to the road passing by
Dirty; and I saw a cockroach in Edwardian Poetry
Reading right to left
Obviously without a library card.

It has been said: "You don't need books any more,
Just boot up and head for GOOGLE!
All that passion, heroism, blood...
Consumptive pens in draughty garrets
Dreaming of flowered fields and yearning for freedom
As they sat in their consumption and dying.
Alcoholics pounding on old Remingtons, with
Chesterfields hanging from dried lips, singing
About lights brighter than the sun.
Printed pages, dog-eared, where ink has come from veins;
Books to take you to wondrous and dark places
Where you can make promises to love and life and honor.

Knowledge has been set upon by the new Huns;
Has been beaten and castrated.
What remains is only information.

Fr. Bob Phelps

Rue

Woman of Sorrows
Ophelia
drowned hair floating among the weeds

slashing with her jagged edges
the drums talked in her bones
but she couldn't interpret
what they said

she'd loved the world once
so Alive
        everything Wild
gripped tightly between thighs
but that last time
        the last time
they made love heavy & slow
like people under water
breathless

tied to the turning wheel
she knew
that no one is remembered
that they always carry their own tombstones
inside them

Do you feel the vastness though?
And just how fleeting every moment is?

the moon a thread of light against the sky
lightning dancing on the horizon
gone beyond gone
she could still move mountains

the moments of a life preserved in stone
grass grown mound
        faded inscription
the cost of freedom
        buried
                in the ground

Pamela Twining

The Circus

Oh the sights before me,
I am cautious
And our sanctioned, calculated words
Woo me into the illusion.

The fanfare is fallacious
I am a spectator pulled from the crowd
To be sawed in half, not by the magician
But a jester and his fools.

We move in circles,
Ravens and the Vulture
The cool wind cuts through the heated tent.
It is twilight and the spotlights ignite

A focal point, your hypersensitivity
Discordant music dizzies my senses
The confusion intoxicating
As you spin me in a box.

Your assistants are ex-lovers and naive recruits
Triangulation squared
With a carefully timed glance
Held for 3...2...1...

You hold two blades
One sharp, one dull
Plunging phantasmagorically
Through my serenity
And I love the complexity of your cuts

Enter the clowns
And all their painted smiles
Fumbling and falling
To witness an assassination of character

Blood on your hands and apron
The wild satisfaction, the predatory pulsing
Leaves your pristine face
You stand hard and aghast

I was always in on this trick
Kill the music. I am still whole.

Tara Yetter

Then He Begged Me to Go Back with Him and Rescue the Others

The essence of a crime never makes the news,
isn't written about in the autopsy report,
or entered into evidence.
The true crime spreads like ripples
after a rock skips across still water,
the lake by the house where he killed her.

Think about the mothers,
the one who carried the murdered
and the one who carried the murderer.
Imagine cradling the weight of their losses.
Then there is the question of forgiveness,
a dozen paper rafts left on the surface
in hopes one may make it to the other side.

The rock thrown is forgotten
long before the water settles,
like prisoners descending into the murky depths
of the system. Every inmate is someone's child,
sibling, cousin, parent, so is every victim.
A rock is a rock is an overused metaphor
for someone who is strong. I am not
a rock. I am the u in True Crime.

If you are brazen enough to ask how my brother
could have committed such a heinous act,
I wouldn't discuss mental illness,
even though I really, really want to
understand.

Instead, I will tell you that when he was eight
and I was fifteen, I spent twenty-two dollars
of my babysitting money
to win him a goldfish at the carnival
and then on our way home,
with tears in his eyes, he knelt beside a small pond,
opened up the plastic bag and set the prisoner free.

Rebecca Schumejda

When Wind is not Enough

Rebecca Schumejda

My mother's
bones are the cross spar
and spine, her skin wrinkled Mylar.
A kite flown from cell to cell, how should the
mother of a prisoner sleep, lights on or off? The truth
is the tale gets tangled around all sorts of misunderstandings.
The message read by men starved of touch. The lights in prison and
my mother's bedroom are always on. If he was your child,
you would not be able to make sense of this either.
Feeling sorry for yourself is not a punishable
offense. I put her to bed, but she forgets,
how I close the window gently
before I bring her flesh
right down into
my hands
as

not

to

allow

her

to

slam

into

the

Addison Goodson

Striding.

Striding 'cross these mountains,,
old and crook-ed
as a tree,
boots
part elk
part human bone,
time my only partner,
blood my only
intermittent feast,
there is quiet,
cold as my stare,
dead as these stars,
alive as the sun
and wind,
the journey never tires
of dragging me along,
towards
truth,
as bare as teeth,
a grin,
a snarl,
to bite us all

PoetryPrompt.com

Create a poem about Breaking News on CNN right now.
But in yours make sure it's raining.

Contemplate the nape of your neck.
Write a sonnet on why it's like the back of the moon:
    a sestet on shape
    a sestet holding your head aloft as allegory
    a heroic couplet that shivers electric between nape and lips

Ekphrasis! Ecstatics! Exclamations!
In sotto voce

Take a class in whole hog butchery
Dedicate it to the one that got away
in iambic pentameter

Write a poem from back to front
so the title surprises you

Do not write haiku
that do not sing from silence
Counting is easy

Pare your skin slowly
with an OXO fruit peeler
until you get to your heart
Write a poem bound by blood splatter

Flip the pages in your desktop planner
Write a poem in the meter of passing time

Without a word
kiss your love
The poem ends when you next inhale

Advice to a Young Poet from your Uncle in Canarsie

Make your poetry a knuckle ball thrown by God
or a drunken butterfly skipping across goldenrods.

Let it be a love note to light playing puppetry in fog
or the anarchist's prayers in a brown paper bag.

Bitterness lurks in the corners, goaded by suicide,
so trust yourself to go ten rounds with the shadows.

Pack each punch with the kiss of delight &
bribe angels to bring fresh salts to your side.

Sure, poetry always has room for bouquets &
ballerinas & often gets kidnapped by balloons,

but it peels the scab off a lie & gives truth its bite.
The MC hears you, so declare love & war at the mic.

The furnace that forged your heart may have died,
but go ahead, break your oath to the horizon & fly.

Career Advice from Your Uncle in Canarsie

Don't sacrifice your dog's testicles or
give your life to selling cookies & tires.
Don't cook the coyote who sang for justice
& definitely don't wear a paste-on mustache
to an office party hosted by a boss who buys
his pants at Sears & drinks pink cocktails with
somebody's college-age daughter from Phoenix.
The Queen of Siam in your needle isn't a sermon.
You'd be surprised what they'll pay for a bucket
of worms if you catch the tides right at the pier.
There's always truth to be dragged from the bottom.
Work hard. Work often. Always collect on Fridays.
Otherwise, I'd offer advice, but I'm no paragon
of employment. When the Episcopalian says,
"I'll sell you another," just stand on the pier
to accept the stink washed up from Long Island.
Your wife wants a new Fuller Brush Man.
Remember, Lent never stopped suicides
& Valentines always wear fangs.
Batteries cost extra, but are required.

Will Nixon with Mike Jurkovic

Family Tree

I don't have a family tree
I have a pile of sticks
And bags of random lawn clippings
Cigarette butts tossed out of windows
By stand-in parents
And other assorted,
Temporary place holders

Empty bottles on the table
In place of family portraits
Everyone has their own
Story to tell
Every sip
A memory
Every glass shard
On the floor
A reminder
That nobody stays too long

Listerine

The smell of Listerine on my father's breath meant
he was heading off to work for the day

That same smell of mouth wash on my mother's breath meant
dad was on his way and it was time to hide the evidence.

She wore perfume to mask what
she was up to while he was gone

He chain-smoked with the windows up in his car
to hide another woman's scent

He showers before and after all his appointments
and he is never clear as to where he's been
you can only golf so many days a week
without being on the PGA tour

She scrubs her flesh under scalding water
trying to get to the clean parts and reclaim that fresh innocence
each time she strays away
physically or not

She never wants this to end
this is what she has been told is right and true
she is meant to be here waiting for him, hoping for more

He never wants this to end
this is what he's been telling her is right and true
he is destined for greatness and she must be ready for the ride

Thom Francis

Her Lot

for Lucy Francois Hymes

The black loamy hole dug for her,
the one everyone said was her place,
her lot in life: How do you fill a hole
when you stand at the bottom
muddy waters rising up.
You grab hold of whatever
you can, especially if it looks solid
like something you can stand on.
Something that just might hold
your weight.

All she had was a fistful of prayer, but
she had outgrown the steeple game,
hands-clasped together turned outside in,
wiggly fingers were the congregation.
She had no time for a faith
that wiggled and squirmed. She
needed blessed assurance.

The preacher said, Build on solid rock.
She said, Amen, rose to her feet,
her arms stretched up; her hands
felt a change in the air, something
clean and cool touched her. Above
her head she heard music in the air.

Her uncle, the one who stepped up and out
onto a diamond. He played black ball, in the game
where only the ball was white. He preached
a different resurrection sermon:
Own your own. A man can stand tall
on his own land. Standing firm against
the wind, he bought buildings
no much to look at, but when he climbed
to the roof, he stood astride the city of big shoulders
its streets and yards at his feet.

She and her man bought a little
piece of land, not even an acre.
The deed they signed called it
a lot. This little piece of land
was their chosen lot. When flood waters
rose, they knew what to do to raise
their lot above the muddy brown waters.
Dump truck after dump truck
Of river sand until their lot
was truly land they could stand on.

The Poets

Editor, Roger Aplon, has published thirteen books: Most recently: *Mustering What's Left – Selected & New Poems – 1976 – 2017* from Unsolicited Press. He lives in Beacon, N Y & publishes the poetry magazine: "Waymark – Voices of the Valley." You can read and hear examples of his work at: rogeraplon.com

Catherine Arra is the author of three chapbooks and two full-length collections, *Writing in the Ether* (Dos Madres Press, 2018), and *Women in Parentheses*, forthcoming from Kelsay Books in 2019. Catherine was a first-time feature for CAPS at Roost Studios and Art Gallery in June 2018. She is most grateful for all CAPS does to promote local literary communities in a variety of venues throughout the area. Arra is a native of the Hudson Valley, where she teaches part-time, and facilitates local writing groups. Find her at catherinearra.com

Scott Bankert: I am a husband, father, friend– a teacher, traveler, and tinkerer. And yet somehow, in spite of everything, I am also a writer. In fact, to call myself a writer would be to refer to my most native self, that part which cannot be removed or extinguished. For me, the words are always already there, fluttering in among the branches – ready to penetrate the secret inner orbits of things. Shy and even self-conscious about my writing (as if it were a condition), it was a great gift to discover CAPS and to have the opportunity to read my poems for the first time to a welcoming audience of peers. CAPS offered to me (an outsider) a warm and lively place to be my native self – a poet among poets.

Eddie Bell is a poet of broad spectrum whose writings speak to everyday people. His four volumes of poetry address the human condition from an African American prospective. His poems cut against the grain of the ordinary and delve into history and society as it relates to the black experience while not neglecting the beauty that surrounds him, both natural and human. His latest collection, *Recrudescence*, is an inward look into the sensitivities of an aging poet.

Mark Blackford was born and grew up in Monticello, NY. He first stumbled across Mike Jurkovic at a poetry reading for a local high school. Being the nice guy he is, Mike invited Mark to come along to some CAPS events in Beacon, eventually inviting him to feature, first in 2014 and again in 2017 (or 2016; time's a blur).

Marianna Boncek grew up in the Catskill Mountains and now lives in the Hudson Valley where she lives and writes with her partner, Dave. She is in her third decade of teaching. She loves attending CAPS where all voices are equally heard.

Frank Boyer began writing poetry in his early 20's, and has, one way or another, kept his hand in ever since. In the 1980's, he participated in the performance art scene in New York City. He moved upstate in 1992, and stopped looking back a long time ago. At CAPS he found poetic rigor, a welcoming spirit, and true friendship. It has been an important home base for him, for many years.

Penny Wickham Brodie is a licensed speech language pathologist. She hosts "Mingus Moments" on WVKR 91.3FM. The inaugural Poet Laureate of Sullivan County, NY.

Timothy Brennan: A poet painter and woodworker, I've lived and worked in Providence, San Francisco, Brooklyn, and now New Paltz, NY, where I've been renovating an old house for almost thirty years with no end in sight. I am interested in language drawn from observation, outside sources (collage, ambient speech and sound, some chance operations) and the meditative interior, twisting and juxtaposing words and syntax to restart perception.

Dennis Wayne Bressack, retired dentist, lives in Woodstock with his wife, Abby. They have two sons, Justin and Noah. He was a member of "Voices in the Valley", the precursor of CAPS. Dennis has featured at many venues, including Howland Cultural Center and Snyder's Estate, ("The Cave"). At the yearly CAPS "Marathon," he has traditionally been the first poet. His work has appeared in many publications and can be found on his website, denniswaynebressack.com

Laurence Carr is an award-winning author and educator. Two poetry collections, *Threnodies* and *The Wytheport Tales* are published by Codhill Press, where he works as editor. His novel, *Pancake Hollow Primer*, won a Next Generation Indie Book Award. Over 20 plays have been produced throughout the U.S. and Europe including *Baklava*, now archived at WNYC radio. Laurence taught creative and dramatic writing at SUNY New Paltz for over twenty years. carrwriter.com

Lucia Cherciu is a Professor of English at Dutchess Community College in Poughkeepsie, New York, and the author of five books of poetry, including *Train Ride to Bucharest* (Sheep Meadow Press, 2017, which received the Eugene Paul Nassar Poetry Prize. Currently she is working on a novel. She is grateful for the support and kindness of the CAPS team. Her web page is luciacherciu.webs.com.

Susan Chute is a librarian and poet who read at the CAPS marathon reading in August 2013, soon after she moved from NYC to New Paltz, and has remained grateful for its embracing and exuberant celebration of poetry ever since. She founded and hosts the New Paltz literary reading series Next Year's Words, and was recently published in *La Presa* and in the Codhill Press anthology *Reflecting Pool: Poets and the Creative Process*.

Michael Sean Collins is a New York based actor, poet and performance artist. His written work has been published in newspapers, magazines and anthologies. He has performed on television, film and radio, in addition to acting in Off-Broadway and regional theater productions throughout the United States and Canada

Richard T. Comerford has read at Word of Mouth Poetry series, Harmony Café Poetry Reading, Mudd Puddle, amongst others. Mike Jurkovic is a good host and I find it very comfortable reading there. I've read there twice. The Marathon is fun because one can hang out as long as there are readers. PS: they have a good snack table.

Greg Correll, CAPS Board member, was a Fellow at the CUNY Writers Institute in 2017, where he worked closely with Leo Carey (*The New Yorker*) and Jonathan Galassi (*FSG*). Wrote about his Parkinson's diagnosis (Salon), and sexual assaults in jail at 14 (Medium). In a half-dozen essay/poetry anthologies, including *Into Sanity* (2019), co-edited by Mark Vonnegut. Two short plays produced, one off-Broadway. A freelance editor, he loves helping writers improve and polish. Three ferocious, brilliant daughters.

Teresa Costa is the poetry hostess with the mostess at Word oF Mouth Poetry Series, held at Artbar Gallery in Kingston, NY. Costa has been writing reading performing her poems since 1974. Costa is married to Richard T. Comerford. CAPS: 20 years is a long time. Ive always had great experiences meeting & hearing other poets at this fantastic venue & it's one of the few that put you so totally at ease.

Ruth Danon is the author *Word Has It, Limitless Tiny Boat,* and *Triangulation From a Known Point*. Her work has been published widely in the United States and abroad and anthologized in *Best American Poetry*, *Resist Much, Obey Little*, and *NOON, An Anthology of the Small Poem*. Shortly after moving to Beacon, NY she was introduced to Mike Jurkovic by their publisher. That was a fortuitous meeting, followed by happy lunches and conversations about CAPS and poetry.

Davida is an Eclectic, living at the edge of what remains of our Catskillian mountain wilderness. Her writings have been published locally and out there internationally. Self-publishing spontaneous yet thoughtful blurts on her Facebook page, she also cameos at public readings; Caps always being a quality excursion. Her material traverses realms from the immaterial worldly to the child's heartbeat and the mundane moonlight through the eyes of the ancestors... as does her form and voice.

Joann K. Deiudicibus (MA, English 2003) teaches writing at SUNY New Paltz. Her poems and articles about poetry appear in *WaterWrites, A Slant of Light, & Reflecting Pool* (Codhill Press), *Chronogram, Affective Disorder and the Writing Life* (Palgrave Macmillan). She's been reading poetry out loud in bars, coffee houses, motels, and churches since her late teens, including the Calling All Poets series. Joann's recently returned to CAPS, and feels grateful for communities like this that foster compassion through art.

Jim Eve is the originator of the Calling All Poets Inc. Calling All Poets was a program that originated at the Howland Cultural Center when Jim was a board member there back in 1999. Along the way he partnered with Mike Jurkovic and together with the help of long time supporters move the program forward. The program obtained its own non-profit status in June of 2014 and currently resides at the Roost Gallery and Studio in New Paltz, NY. Jim, who writes poetry whenever the mood strikes him, considers himself more of a facilitator of poetry than a poet.

Karen Fabiane been writing, performing, and publishing poetry (small press) since the 1970s; 2 chapbooks in print: *Dancing Bears* (Bright Hill Press) & *Seeing You Again* (Grey Book Press). She has read numerous places, but experience with CAPS is limited to 2/3 events (+ cancelled-due-to weather feature, 1/18). The community seems very enthusiastic & integrated; She likes the informal atmosphere. Always appreciated opportunity to read @ CAPS..

Sharon Ferrante: When I discovered CAPS, my love of poetry was rekindled. With their dedication to welcoming you, I feel a belonging. Like a brushstroke from the colorful palette of the spoken word. Showing kindness of diversity, a collage of Hudson Valley Awe. As they give of their time, an encouraged poet hears a little song. Thank you CAPS, a jaw-dropper, recommended to all!

Louisa Finn: The daughter of a classical pianist and a physical therapist, Louisa has always written but only recently dared to call herself poet. She has a career as a speech/language therapist and reading tutor for dyslexics and lives in High Falls, NY where she and her husband have raised two solid, whole-hearted boys.

Thom Francis is the president of Albany Poets and has been organizing, promoting, and hosting open mics and poetry / spoken word events in Albany such as *Nitty Gritty Slam, School of Night, Albany Poets Presents*, and the *Albany Word Fest* for over 13 years. As a poet and performer, Thom has been featured at many of the upstate poetry and spoken word events from Saratoga to Woodstock to New Paltz as well as *LarkFest, Art on Lark, 1st Friday*, and the *Albany Word Fest*.

Lewis Gardner's poems and plays have been published throughout the U.S., including more than 60 poems in the *New York Times* and several plays distributed through One Act Play Depot. He is also an actor and a teacher of writing. He's grateful for the opportunity CAPS has provided to read to a responsive audience.

Leslie Gerber, born in Brooklyn 1943, graduated from Brooklyn College, escaped from NY in 1970, in Ulster County ever since. Ran a classical music mail order business for 39 years, wrote thousands of reviews. Still publishing classical CDs. Third book, *Losing Tara: An Alzheimer's Journey* due out summer 2019. Featured at CAPS twice, read in open mic too many times for comfort. CAPS is so ambitious I'm glad I don't have to run it.

Addison Goodson, born in New York City, organized progressive voters in Venice, California, fought against Apartheid at UCLA, flew all over this world, lives to work with my sisters and brothers to preserve life, peace and justice on this lovely planet EARTH.

Shotsie Gorman: Arts educator, poet, 41 year professional tattoo artist, Alliance of Professional Tattooists, journalist, publisher, owner of Tarot Art & Tattoo Gallery. Exhibiting myriad art forms: watercolors, abstract ceramics, oils on canvas, acrylic abstractions. Art on exhibit in museums and galleries around the world. Poet doing live performances and ESL workshops. Author of poetry collection "The Black Marks He Made" published Proteus Press.

Janet Hamill is the author of eight books of poetry and short fiction. Her MFA in Creative Writing/Poetry is from New England College. Presently, she serves as Director of Megaphone Language Arts at the Seligmann Center in Sugar Loaf, NY.

Steve Hirsch is the former editor/publisher of *Heaven Bone* magazine. He studied poetics and theatre at Naropa University in Boulder, CO, where he was an apprentice to Allen Ginsberg and Chogyam Trungpa Rinpoche. Steve is the author of *Ramapo 500 Affirmations* (Flower Thief, 1998) and he has appeared in *Hunger, Napalm Health Spa Report, Pudding* ,and *Big Scream* among others. Steve has read numerous times at CAPS and feels he has given some of his best readings in our venue.

Ken Holland: When I recently featured at The Roost, I shared that CAPS is my poetic home. And how when I judge certain poems to be worthy enough, I keep on ice until I have the chance to give them their first airing in New Paltz. The steady caliber of work presented at the monthly readings is the best in the valley. If this sounds more like a biography of CAPS than myself, that's wholly appropriate.

Susan Hoover has featured at The New School, The Knitting Factory, The Kitchen, The Cornelia Street Café and throughout the Hudson Valley. Her work has appeared in *Cold Mountain Review, Isinglass Review, University of Colorado Literary Magazine, Home Planet News, Chronogram,* and *Granite*. Her books include *The Magnet* and *The Target* (New School Chapbook Series, 1995), *Taxi Dancer* (Exotic Beauties Press, 1979), and her latest, *The Mathematics of Disengagement* (Post Traumatic Press, 2017)

Matthew Hupert is the founder of the NeuroNautic Press. He is the author of Secular Pantheism (2019), *Ism is a Retrovirus* (2011), several chapbooks, and has appeared widely in journals and anthologies including *Midstream Magazine*, the DaDa journal *Maintenant*, and Sonnets: *150 Contemporary Sonnets* (2005). Matthew hosts the annual showcase for NYC voices, *Night in the Naked City*, and the monthly series *NeuroNautic Institute Presents*.

Kate Hymes, poet, workshop leader and writing consultant, lives in New Paltz, New York. She has nurtured writers in the Hudson Valley through her leadership of Wallkill Valley Writers. Kate's recent publication is a chapbook, True Grain. Published in three regional anthologies edited by Codhill Press: *Riverine: An Anthology of Hudson Valley Writers, Slant of Light: Contemporary Women Writers of the Hudson Valley,* and *Reflecting Pool: Poets and the Creative Process*—and *Gathering Ground: Cave Canem 10 Year Anniversary Anthology*, University of Michigan Press. Kate edited *wVw Anthologies 2011* and *2015*, containing memoir, short fiction and poetry.

Mike Jurkovic is President, Calling All Poets. 2016 Pushcart nominee. Full length titles: *Blue Fan Whirring, smitten by harpies,* & *shiny banjo catfish.* Chapbook: *Eve's Venom.* Anthologies: *Reflecting Pool: Poets & the Creative Process, WaterWrites: A Hudson River Anthology,* and *Riverine: Anthology of Hudson Valley Writers* (Codhill Press, 2018, 2009, 2007) Features and CD reviews appear in *All About Jazz, Van Wyck Gazette, Maverick Chronicles.* He is the Tuesday night host of Jazz Sanctuary, WOOC 105.3 FM, Troy, NY.
He loves Emily most of all. mikejurkovic.com

Alison Koffler writes mostly about humans and other animals. The four-time winner of the Bronx Council on the Arts' BRIO Award, she appreciates greatly what CAPS has in support of Hudson Valley poetry. Alison lives in the Bronx and Woodstock, NY with the poet Dayl Wise and their dog Cole. She's the co-founder of *Post Traumatic Press*.

Ron Kolm is a contributing editor of *Sensitive Skin*. Ron is the author of *Night Shift, A Change in the Weather,* and *Welcome to the Barbecu*e. Ron's papers are archived in the New York University library. I read at the Roost Studios in New Paltz, New York. I was invited to read by Mike Jurkovic, and I am grateful to have gotten a grant from CAPS for that event.

Susan Konz's work has appeared in *The Waymark* and *CAPS Anthology 2015*. She is a featured contributor to the Calling All Poets Writing Series based in New Paltz, NY. She received her MFA from Hunter College and currently works as an editor for *I Want You to See This Before I Leave*, an online poetry zine. Her first book, *Second Sleep*, was published in 2016 with Lion Autumn Publishing. She is currently working on a new collection.

Raphael Kosek's poems have appeared in such venues as *Poetry East, Catamaran,* and *Briar Cliff Review*. Her latest chapbook, *Rough Grace*, won the 2014 Concrete Wolf Chapbook Prize. Her new book, *American Mythology*, will be released in 2019. She has been a supporter of CAPS since their genesis and feels they have contributed to both her own growth as a poet and the very rich poetry culture blooming in the Hudson Valley. She teaches English at Marist College and Dutchess Community College in the Hudson Valley where her students keep her real. She is the 2019 Dutchess County Poet Laureate.

Linda Lerner's recent collections: *A Dance Around the Cauldron*, (Lummox press, 2017) *Yes, The Ducks Were Real* (NYQ Books, 2015;) *Taking the F Train* is forthcoming from NYQ Books. In spring, 2015 she read six poems on WBAI. In 1995 she and Andrew Gettler began *Poets on the Line* (echony.com/~poets).

Jared Levine has been active in the Hudson Valley scene since 2016, having published in that time: two book-length collections of poems and prose, hosted a monthly open-mic series, and participated at dozens of other series and events. Calling All Poets features some of the region's finest writers; it is an honor to share their company in these pages. Congratulations on twenty excellent, innovative years – and cheers to the future, sure to contain many more.

Mary Makofske was born and grew up in Washington, DC. She worked as a travel agent, news and feature writer, and health educator before becoming an English professor at SUNY Orange (aka OCCC), from which she retired in 2006. Her latest books are *World Enough, and Time* (Kelsay, 2017) and *Traction* (Ashland, 2011), winner of the Richard Snyder Prize.

John Martucci is a songwriter, which led him to poetry and CAPS by way of Mike Jurkovic, his co-writer. His poems, like his songs, are short and simple. Mike got him interested in writing poetry, and he eventually persuaded him to put aside his shyness and read at CAPS. By coming to CAPS and hearing so many poetic voices, John has grown in poetic skill and confidence.

Marina Mati's publications include the *Napalm Health Spa; BigCityLit; Waymark*, and several anthologies including the *Wawayanda Review*. She has enjoyed being the featured poet throughout NYC and the Hudson Valley. In the West Village, she co-hosted a poetry series featuring future literary notables such as Sapphire and Hal Sirowitz. She is the editor of the first *CAPS Poetry Anthology* put out in 2015. Her chapbook, *cave-speak*, will again be available after being revised and expanded. Marina enjoys an occasional gig as an actor and, on Sundays, joins the drum circle in the town's village green.

Mary Newell is the author of the chapbook *TILT/ HOVER/ VEER* (Codhill Press 2019) and poems in a number of journals. Dr. Newell has taught literature and writing at the college level. She lives in the lower Hudson River valley and curates the Hudson Highlands Poetry Series in Garrison. Website: manitoulive.wixsite.com/maryn

Will Nixon has published poetry and books about Woodstock co-authored with Michael Perkins. His most memorable reading at CAPS came about thanks to Mike Jurkovic with whom he collaborated on a number of poems. He couldn't even remember which lines had originally been Mike's and which his. Will Nixon's most recent book, *Acrostic Woodstock*, is a portrait of the town in poems.

Irene O'Garden has won or been nominated for prizes in nearly every writing category from stage to e-screen, hardcovers, children's book, including receiving The Pushcart Prize for her lyrical essay, "Glad to Be Human." Her critically-acclaimed *Women on Fire* played to sold-out houses at Off-Broadway's Cherry Lane Theatre. Other books include *Fat Girl* (Harper) and *Fulcrum: Selected Poems* (Nirala) Her newest memoir is *Risking the Rapids: How My Wilderness Adventure Healed My Childhood* (Mango, 2019) ireneogarden.com

Fr. Bob Phelps is a Franciscan Capuchin friar who began writing creatively while on private retreat in a rain forest on Maui, in 1991. His work has appeared in many poetry journals, such as the *Evansville Review* and the *Nassau Review*. He joined the Calling All Poets in the spring of 2012, and shares his work in the local poetry community when he is able.

For over thirty years writer/journalist **Fred Poole** traveled throughout the world's dangerous territories – Haiti, Cuba, Beirut, Angola, Kuala Lampur – and published over a dozen books including *Where Dragons Dwell* (Harper) and *Revolution in the Philippines: the U.S. in a Hall of Cracked Mirrors* (McGraw-Hill). Drawing from his experiences as a writer, teacher, artist and seeker, he created the Authentic Writing Workshops in 1993. Fred runs workshops regularly in Woodstock, Manhattan, and Omega Institute. He wrote *Authentic Writing, A Memoir on Creating Memoir* in 2008.

Guy Reed is co-author, with Cheryl A. Rice, of the chapbook, *Until The Words Came* (2019 Post Traumatic Press). In 2018, he co-wrote and directed the short film, *How The World Looks Now*. He's author of *The Effort To Hold Light* (Post Traumatic Press). Guy has read at CAPS many times. Coming from the eastern Catskills, he considers CAPS a poetic home away from home no matter where it's been housed. Someday, more information at guyedwinreed.com

Donna Reis's debut poetry collection, *No Passing Zone*, published by Deerbrook Editions (December, 2012) was nominated for a Pushcart Prize. She is co-editor and contributor to the anthology, *Blues for Bill: A Tribute to William Matthews* (Akron Poetry Series, 2005). Her non-fiction book, *Seeking Ghosts in the Warwick Valley*, published by Schiffer Publishing, Ltd (2003) has sold nearly 3000 copies.

Cheryl A. Rice's poems have appeared in journals around the world. Chapbooks include *Until the Words Came* (2019: Post Traumatic Press), coauthored with Guy Reed, *Moses Parts the Tulips* (2013: APD Press), and *Lost and Found* (2019: Flying Monkey Press). She is founder/host of the now defunct "Sylvia Plath Bake-Off." Her blog is at: flyingmonkeyprods.blogspot.com. Rice lives in New York's Hudson Valley. CAPS is the latest gang of unsavory poet types she's associated with.

Rayn Roberts: Roost Studio & Art Gallery is a lovely venue with art that adds beautifully to readings. Refreshments are provided. I had a very good time when I featured there on my way to Wales where I was invited to feature on Dylan Thomas' birthday in his old house in Swansea. At home, I'm active in the poetry scene hosting a well-established reading at the Green Lake Branch Seattle Public Library.

Bertha Rogers has been a featured poet at CAPS three times, each time a delight! She has published three collections of poetry, most recently *Wild, Again* (Salmon Poetry, Ireland); and her *Uncommon Creatures: The Riddle-Poems from the Exeter Book Translated and Illuminated* is just out. She lives in the western Catskills, where she co-founded and served as executive director of Bright Hill Press & Literary Center of the Catskills for 25 years.

Judith Saunders is a long-time resident of the Hudson Valley and often writes about the landscapes, weather, flora, fauna, and culture of the region. Her poems have appeared in a wide variety of local and national venues, and she is the author of two prize-winning chapbook collections of poetry.

Rebecca Schumejda is the author of four full-length books: *Falling Forward* (sunnyoutside press), *Cadillac Men* (NYQ Books), *Waiting at the Dead End Diner* (Bottom Dog Press), *Our One-Way Street* (NYQ Books) and the chapbooks: *The Tear Duct of the Storm* (Green Bean Press) *Dream Big, Work Harder* (sunnyoutside press), *The Map of Our Garden* (verve bath press), *From Seed to Sin* (Bottle of Smoke Press) She is the co-author of *Common Wages* with Don Winter (Working Stiff Press).

William Seaton is a poet, translator, and critic who read with Jim Eve and Mike Jurkovic even before Calling All Poets, which they and their colleagues have developed into the region's premiere poetry series. Seaton is the author of *Spoor of Desire: Selected Poems* and *Dada Poetry: An Introduction* and has been active in poetry performance since the sixties. He maintains a largely literary blog at williamseaton.blogspot.com.

A world traveling poetry ambassador, **Yuyutsu Sharma** is a distinguished poet, translator, and recipient of fellowships/grants from The Rockefeller Foundation and the Ireland Literature Exchange. His nine poetry collections include, *A Blizzard in my Bones: New York Poems*, *Quaking Cantos: Nepal Earthquake Poems*, and *Annapurnas Poems*. He is the Visiting Poet at Columbia University as well as editor of *Pratik, A Magazine of Contemporary Writing*.

Gary Siegel: I am a Poet. My writing is driven by journeys into nature as well as the inner journeys. When I found the CAPS, I found an environment. I would say that at CAPs – we take our poetry seriously, but not necessarily ourselves. There is the feeling that the readers here are deeply dug into their craft, while all are welcome and encouraged to work their art. The place has that feel. After a night at the Roost I want to love reading more and I want to get better. I also want very much to come back.

Matthew J. Spireng is a widely published, award-winning poet with two full-length books, *Out of Body* and *What Focus Is*, and five chapbooks to his credit. He has been nominated for the Pushcart Prize eight times. He has been a featured reader for CAPS on several occasions—enough that he can't remember how many, though he does remember enjoying every one, both as a reader and as a listener.

Since leaving the ashram, **Marta Szabo** has scored an MFA in Creative Writing from Goddard College and completed two memoirs, *The Guru Looked Good* and *The Imposters*. She posts current writing at *Experiments in Memoir*. Marta is the co-director of Authentic Writing and teaches the program in colleges and schools throughout the Hudson Valley, as well as to cancer survivors, at-risk teens, and at correctional facilities. She created *Ink in the Air* a radio show for WJFF, in Jeffersonville, NY.

Tim Tomlinson is a co-founder of New York Writers Workshop. His story collection *This Is Not Happening to You* has been likened to "licking something bitter from a very sharp knife." He is the author of the poetry collection, *Requiem for the Tree Fort I Set on Fire*, and *Yolanda: An Oral History in Verse*. He read at CAPS in New Paltz during the Great Freeze of 2019; he continues to thaw in Brooklyn. He teaches in NYU's Global Liberal Studies.

Edwin Torres has read for CAPS in Beacon, NY, at The Howland in 2016 and at The Town Crier in 2019, each time was a warm connection with a very focused audience, a direct reflection of Mike's vibe. Edwin is the author of ten books including, *Xoeteox: the infinite word object* (Wave Books), *Ameriscopia* (University of Arizona Press), *Yes Thing No Thing* (Roof Books) and editor of *The Body In Language: An Anthology* (Counterpath Press).

With her partner, poet Andy Clausen, **Pamela Twining** performs her work throughout the US. Her work has appeared in *Big Scream, PoetryBay, The Café Review, Napalm Health Spa*, and *Heyday!*, among others. With Clausen, she co-curates *The Invisible Empires of Beatitude at T* (poetspath.com). Author of three chapbooks, *i have been a river..., utopians & madmen*, and *A Thousand Years of Wanting; the Erotic Poetry of Pamela Twining*.

Peter Ullian is Poet Laureate for the City of Beacon, NY. His poems have appeared in magazines and anthologies, and been nominated for the Pushcart Prize and the Rhysling Award. His publications include *Secret Histories* and *Exobiologies (The Poet's Haven)* and *The Fevered Dream-Crimes of Pulp-Fiction Poets and Other Love Stories: New and Selected Poems* (Lion Autumn Music Publishing). "Appearing as a featured poet at CAPS allowed my poems come alive and tell a story."

T. G. Vanini is a songwriter, poet and mathematician. His latest album with The Princes of Serendip is *Yumpatiddly Bee: Silly Songs* (Jaiya Records, 2019). His book of poetry, *Dear Cloudface*, was published by Post Traumatic Press in 2018. He is glad to have been part of CAPS's important role in the area's culture, including readings at the beautiful Howland Center in Beacon and the Roost in the heart of New Paltz.

George Wallace is writer in residence at the Walt Whitman Birthplace, author of 34 chapbooks of poetry, and the first American to be awarded the Alexander Gold Medal, UNESCO-Piraeus Islands. Editor of *Poetrybay* and co-editor of *Great Weather for Media*, he lives in New York and travels worldwide to perform his work, including frequent visits to Beacon, Woodstock, and the Hudson Valley.

Glenn Werner is a poet/artist who's work has been published in several publications including: *Chronogram Magazine, The Waywayanda Review, 4th Street, Up the River, A Well Lighted Place, Snow Monkey*, and *Home Planet News*. He was nominated for a Pushcart Prize by Donald Lev of Home Planet News. He has served as Treasurer and Vice-President of CAPS. His poetry collection *From A Mongrel Poet* can be found on Amazon.com

Bruce Weber is the author of five books of poems. As an art historian, he has recently been writing and lecturing about the historic Woodstock art colony.

Greg Wilder is a 30 year old sophomore poet. With 2 years clean, recovery has played a significant role in his writing, and vice versa. Greg began writing and performing poetry in his outpatient treatment center before reading for the first time in public at last year's *Readings Against the End of the World* event. Since then he has performed at many local open-mic venues and slams.

Dayl Wise, a soldier once, returned to Vietnam three times in the1990's with a different mission, delivering medical supplies and coming to terms with his time there as a soldier. Author of two chapbooks of poetry, he lives in Woodstock, NY with his wife, the poet Alison Koffler. He is the co-founder of PostTraumaticPress.com.

Christopher Wheeling has been attending Calling All Poets Series regularly for 17 years. In 2011, he joined the team as photographer, documenting the series for future posterity and/or notoriety. He's been published in *Home Planet News*, *Chronogram*, *The Waywayanda Review*, *Waymark*, *Voices From Here: The Paulinskill Poetry Project Volume II*, *Calling All Poets Series Anthology 2015*, and *The Stillwater Review*. CAPS has changed significantly since he joined, and he looks forward to the future.

R. Dionysius Whiteurs: Born in the Bronx. Raised in the Bronx and Mahwah, NJ. Ron (R. Dionysius) Whiteurs has lived in the New Paltz-Rosendale area since 1966. MA in English SUNY NP. Unofficial poet laureate of IBM Publishing 1980-1990. Performed at many venues and events in the Midhudson area. Also performed at Fountain House, the Nuyorican, Out Loud Festival, Steve Charney Show ("Knock-On-Wood") on WAMC Radio, Woodstock Guild and many other places and events.

Walter Worden's poems have appeared in numerous publications such as *Chronogram*, *The First Literary Review*, *Home Planet News* and *The Literary Gazette*. His work was also included in a special presentation on The Huffington Post website, as well as featured on Jonathan Wolfman's podcasts "Passionate Justice" and "Lit Snips". Worden is a former host of a reading and performance series, and has published a collection of poems entitled *This land and Every Stone*. A second book is due to be published in the summer of 2019.

Tara Yetter was the host of two poetry reading series in Milford, Pennsylvania for seven years. Her poetry is dark, abstract, and rich with imagery. She has been a featured poet throughout the tristate area including the Calling All Poets reading series. It is a supportive and challenging environment that has personally inspired her to be a better poet. She currently lives in a forest in Pennsylvania and is working on a collection of short stories.

Made in the USA
Middletown, DE
23 November 2019